RECENT DISCOVERIES AND THE BIBLICAL WORLD

RECENT DISCOVERIES AND THE BIBLICAL WORLD

Raymond E. Brown, S.S.

Wipf and Stock Publishers
EUGENE, OREGON

Wipf and Stock Publishers
199 West 8th Avenue, Suite 3
Eugene, Oregon 97401

Recent Discoveries and the Biblical World
By Brown, Raymond E.
Copyright©1983 by Brown, Raymond E.
ISBN: 1-59244-351-6
Publication date 9/18/2003
Previously published by Michael Glazier, Inc., 1983

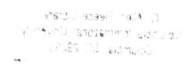

Acknowledgments

The publisher gratefully gives credit to the following copyright holders for the illustrations used in this book: *Biblical Archaeologist* (courtesy of): Ebla tablets, page 23. Oriental Institute of the University of Chicago: Nuzi Tablet, page 30; Table showing the development of cuneiform script, page 32; Stele of Mesha, page 36; Stables at Megiddo, page 61. The British Museum: Codex Sinaiticus, page 47. Israel Government Tourist Office (courtesy of): Wall of Jericho, page 55. United Press International: A man's posture on cross, page 80. Israel Government, Department of Antiquities and Museum (courtesy of): Spike-pierced heel bone, page 81. Benjamin Mazar (courtesy of): Artist's sketch of temple mount, page 86. Israel Exploration Society: Herodian pavement and steps, page 87.

Typography by Susan Pickett. •   • Cartography by Lucille Dragovan.

TO
THE MEMORY OF
WILLIAM FOXWELL ALBRIGHT
who illustrated for his students
how broad human knowledge can be

Contents

ILLUSTRATIONS

INTRODUCTION

INTRODUCTION

THE BIBLE IS, we believe, the word of God. But a belief in the inspired character of the Bible does not make its pages any less a chronicle of the existence of people: Hebrews, Israel, the Jews,[1] and Christians. Covering almost 2000 years, and consisting of 66 to 73 different books[2] written at widely separate periods of time, the Bible may best be perceived as the preserved library of those people. In particular, the Old Testament was the library of Israel, and the New Testament was the library of the early Church. While every research method that enlightens human activity is capable of throwing light on the Bible, in this little book I shall concentrate on recent discoveries gained mostly through archaeology. "Recent" must be elastic enough to stretch back to the era between the two World Wars, even if most attention is given to the period after the Second War.

[1] A common estimate of the extent of biblical history is from 1850 B.C. to A.D. 150. In the Old Testament period "Israel" is an appropriate title after the affiliation of the twelve tribes; "Jews" is a designation related to the tribe of Judah, the chief survivor of the tribal confederation in the post-exilic period (after 539).

[2] The Hebrew canon, followed by many Protestant Churches, has 39 books; but Jews and Christians group these Old Testament books in a different order. On the basis of Jewish tradition in Alexandria, the Roman Catholic Church and some Orthodox Churches recognize 7 more books, often called deuterocanonical; some Oriental Churches recognize even more. Christians are at one in acknowledging 27 New Testament books.

The discoveries are of two types: *written* material hitherto unknown or unavailable; and *physical* remains of culture, life, and worship. These discoveries pertain to the "biblical world," that is, the world of Israel and the early Christians, but also of other cultures and peoples with whom they came in contact.

Let me explain in a personal way why this study is appearing under the imprint of this publisher and written by me. Michael Glazier came to me some years ago with a plan to publish a *New Testament Message* series, a plan that has been broadened to include an *Old Testament Message* series. The plan was to offer interested readers a distillation of modern biblical scholarship in brief commentaries on the individual books of the Bible. These commentaries were to be accompanied by a few booklets on general topics that readers need to know by way of introduction to biblical studies. (A superb example of the latter is Daniel J. Harrington's *Interpreting the New Testament* which is a survey of the different ways in which scholars approach the Bible.) I encouraged him in the project because I think it an essential religious duty to make respectable and reliable biblical knowledge available to the non-specialist. It is one way of protecting ordinary Jews and Christians from the malady of biblical fundamentalism of which I shall speak presently. It is a way to open their minds to the challenge of the living God. Nevertheless, as I watched the project unfold I noticed a gap to which I was particularly sensitive because of my own life experience — the series did not have a general work on how archaeological discoveries have cast light on the biblical world.

I thought back on how I became interested in the Bible. For a student in a college seminary it was a mandated religious exercise to read through the Bible cover to cover. For the first time in my life, on a schedule of ten minutes a day, I worked through this tremendous collection of books, truly moved by the insights I found there. I can still remember stopping for a long time at Genesis 29:20, "Jacob worked seven years for [the privilege of marrying] Rachel, and they seemed to him but a few days because of the greatness of his love." Nothing I had ever read explained better how I might approach the long years of seminary preparation for the service of Christ. When I entered formal theological studies in Rome, I had to learn Italian; and so I read a history of Israel in that language. I had always loved history, and this book (although not extraordinarily competent) opened for me the understanding of how what I had read spiritually might be fitted into the panorama of the human story. It was the beginning of an insight that has remained precious to me ever since. I had taken on faith that the word of God was truly "of God," but now I began to understand that "word" was something spoken by human beings living in circumstances that marked and qualified the expression. My next step was to work through a few major biblical books accompanied by a brief commentary.

Nevertheless, it took one more ingredient to make me decide that I would like to spend my life studying the Bible. That came when I read C. C. McCown, *Ladder of Progress in Palestine* (New York: Harper, 1943). It was an attractively written account of how archaeological discoveries of documents and sites since the nineteenth century have thrown light on the Bible. Through that book it became clear to me that we were living in a privileged era when the great development of human knowledge of our times, namely, science, was making its contribution toward our understanding of God. (I had no illusions then or since that scientific knowledge is the supreme form of knowledge; it is the limited contribution of this era to the totality of knowledge. But for Christians to ignore what science can contribute would be a tragedy no less serious than if the early Church Fathers had refused to employ philosophy in their attempts to understand Jesus of Nazareth.) I became more convinced of this as I read other books on the archaeology of Egypt and of Mesopotamia, the world empires between which Canaan or Palestine was a buffer state. Still later I discovered serious geographical science in Denis Baly's *Geography of the Bible* (New York: Harper, 1957). All this convinced me that it was necessary for anyone who wished to read the Bible intelligently to know something of the civilizations and lands in which the people of God, old and new, lived. Otherwise one might miss the fact that the Bible was a human word of the almighty God catching in itself all the mystery of the incarnation — of the divine in the human.

I did my doctoral studies in the 1950s under the man whom many judge the greatest biblical archaeologist of the twentieth century, William Foxwell Albright of The Johns Hopkins University. My doctoral dissertation, *The Semitic Background of the Pauline* Mystērion, was a testimony that even "the mystery which has been hidden from the ages in the God who created all things" had a detectable human context which contributed to and modified its expression. When I worked on *The Jerome Biblical Commentary* (Englewood Cliffs, NJ: Prentice Hall, 1968) it was by my choice that I edited the article on biblical archaeology and co-authored the article on biblical geography. And so when the executive editor of *The Great Ideas Today* (the annual supplement to the *Encyclopaedia Britannica*), John Van Doren, phoned and asked me to write on "Recent Contributions to Our Knowledge of the Bible," I leaped at the chance to bring together in concise form a branch of biblical knowledge that had been a passion for me since seminary days. What is contained in this book is an adapted form of what appeared in the 1982 *Great Ideas Today*, pp. 104-57.

I have offered it to Michael Glazier as a companion to the *Message* series of commentaries with two hopes. The first is the somewhat romantic possibility that what moved me to a lifetime commitment to biblical studies might work the same magic for others. I do not mean that I wish to inflate beyond reason the tribe of professional biblical scholars, but only to increase the number of passionate students of the Bible. (And, indeed, as I move around the country I meet many avid readers of the Bible, not fundamentalist at all, who do not have the formal education to become professional scholars but whose enthusiastic devotion would put many biblical scholars to shame.)

My second hope is not romantic but deadly serious. I hope that even a basic acquaintance with the civilizations that were the contexts of the biblical writers will lead to thoughtful reflection on how those civilizations conditioned the expression of the word of God. Whatever "fundamentalism" meant at its origin, the term now describes a mindset wherein the expression of divine revelation is thought not to be time-conditioned. For most fundamentalists unconditioned revelation is found in the Bible; for some Roman Catholics it is enshrined in the decrees of their Church; for some Jews, I suspect, whether or not they would use the language, it is enshrined in the Torah, the Mishna, or the Talmud. (Incidentally, it should be noted for Roman Catholics that in *Mysterium Ecclesiae* [1973] the Roman Holy Office or Doctrinal Commission stated explicitly that historical condition affects the expression of revelation and that truths are enunciated by the Magisterum in the changeable conceptions of a given epoch.) A religious tragedy resulting from fundamentalism in the biblical sphere is that through it the Bible is brought into irreconcilable conflict with the majority scientific views of our time. For instance, one cannot read Genesis 1-2 as an absolute statement about how God brought into being this world and its inhabitants and still accept evolution. A fundamentalist will reject the sciences that have proposed evolution in favor of the higher truth of the Bible; a religious non-fundamentalist will recognize that the author of Genesis shared the views of his time about the *way* in which God created and will be open to accepting evolution as a more informed view of that way. What the Bible teaches the latter person is that no matter what was the way (which is a question where science has the dominant voice), God was responsible for all. A knowledge of the discoveries I shall discuss below will show how constant a challenge science is to the biblical interpretations of the past and will inculcate caution about glib fundamentalist tendencies to harmonize.

But there is another problem that fundamentalism brings to Christians in particular. Jesus was opposed by religious people who thought fundamentalistically. They thought that their interpretation of the Law was from God and unconditioned. When Jesus violated that interpretation, he was setting himself up against God. (The fact that in the Gospel story these opponents were Jews is, in my opinion, not really important; the religious mindset is the essential issue.) From Jesus' viewpoint their interpretation was a human tradition that was not equatable with the will of God (Matt 15:6) — in other words, a time-conditioned expression of God's will that did not exhaust that will, an expression that rendered service but became destructive when absolutized. How ironic to find a basic insight that justified Jesus' challenge to the people of his time now rejected by fundamentalists who claim to be loyal to him but intellectually would be closer in outlook to those who opposed him. A non-fundamentalist approach to the Bible, distinguishing between the intent of the revelation and the way in which it was phrased because of the circumstances of the biblical period, is possible only if one knows those circumstances. Archaeological discoveries were what first alerted scholars that the Israelites lived, wrote, and thought similarly to the people of the kingdoms that surrounded them. A survey of such discoveries may help the ordinary reader of the Bible to hold on to that essential perception.

For what follows it may be useful to have a chart of the *approximate* datings usually assigned to the eras or ages discussed in archaeology (all dates are B.C.):

Chalcolithic	4000-3150
Early Bronze	3150-2200
EB I	3150-2850
EB II	2850-2700
EB III	2700-2350
EB IV	2350-2200
Middle Bronze	2200-1550
MB I	2200-2000
MB IIA	2000-1750
MB IIB	1750-1550
Late Bronze	1550-1200
LB I	1550-1400
LB IIA	1400-1300
LB IIB	1300-1200
Iron	1200-586
Iron I	1200-1000
Iron II	1000-586

The footnotes are meant to facilitate reading of a less technical character, especially in:

BA   *Biblical Archaeologist* (a quarterly)
BAR   *Biblical Archaeologist Reader* (3 paperback vols.; Garden City, NY: Doubleday, 1961, 1964, 1970)
BARev   *Biblical Archaeology Review* (a bimonthly)

PART I

Discoveries

of

Tablets and Scrolls

Discoveries of Tablets and Scrolls

ONE OF THE WAYS in which our knowledge of the Bible has been greatly expanded is by the discovery of pertinent writings. Sometimes these are copies of biblical books older than any copies hitherto possessed (Dead Sea Scrolls, Bodmer Papyri). Sometimes they are works reflecting biblical religion but not accepted into the canonical collection (Dead Sea Scrolls, Nag Hammadi). More often, the written discoveries cast light on the world in which the biblical peoples lived and on the languages and writing-styles used in the Bible (Ebla, Ugarit, Mari, Nuzi). Empires, peoples, and cities previously little-known have left records (Hittites, Hurrians, Amarna), filling in the background of biblical history. The selection of writings below, meant to illustrate all this, moves in an approximately chronological order from the earliest historical period to the latest.

EBLA

Abraham, Isaac, Jacob, and Joseph are the patriarchs of the Book of Genesis, migrants from Mesopotamia to Canaan, keepers of flocks, and merchants in contact with the kingdoms of Mesopotamia and Egypt. Most scholars would start the patriarchal history in the second millennium B.C. (Middle Bronze IIA by archaeological reckoning), but that is far from certain. Consequently there has been a constant interest of biblical scholars in the great civilizations of the last half of the third millennium (Early Bronze), either as an alternative, earlier setting for the patriarchal period (below, p. 75), or as the forerunner of the second millennium cultures encountered by the patriarchs. A recent discovery has uncovered a major third millennium center in Syria (situated between Hama and Aleppo), closer geographically and linguistically to Canaan than were the Sumerian, Akkadian, and Egyptian civilizations hitherto known. Since 1964 an Italian archaeological mission of the University of Rome directed by Paolo Matthiae has been excavating Tell Mardikh (ancient Ebla), a city with a claimed population of a quarter of a million which was destroyed by Naram-Sin of Akkad, a ruler known already through Mesopotamian finds. In 1974 through 1976 the archives of Ebla came to light — an enormous discovery of over 16,500 inventoried items dating from the period 2400-2250 B.C. The epigrapher of the expedition, Giovanni Pettinato, estimates that 80% of the tablets are in Sumerian, a non-Semitic language of international import, while 20% are in a Semitic language (now dubbed Eblaite), seemingly of the same Northwestern branch as Hebrew.[3] This large tablet-find will be of prime importance for Middle Eastern history, religion, and sociology, as well as for our knowledge of the languages of the region (especially because of the bilingual vocabularies contained therein).

---

[3]Semitic languages are often divided into *Northeastern* (Akkadian, Assyrian, Babylonian), and *Southeastern* (South Arabic, Ethiopic), as distinct from *Northwestern* (Amorite, Canaanite, Aramaic), and *Southwestern* (Arabic). By further specification, the Canaanite sphere includes Ugaritic, Hebrew, and Phoenician. Similar terminology is sometimes applied to the Semitic peoples.

Clay Tablets at Ebla

"In 1974 through 1976 the archives of Ebla came to
light — an enormous discovery of over 16,500 inventoried items dating from the period 2400-2250 B.C."

An acrimonious debate has taken place between Matthiae and Pettinato[4] over the import of the tablets for the Bible, the earliest passages of which date over 1000 years later. It is a major difficulty that the cuneiform (wedge-shaped) signs used in Eblaite writing are capable of being read with several different equivalences. Nevertheless, in two directions the discovery promises to have biblical significance. *First,* over 10,000 personal names appear in these tablets, which are largely commercial; and some of them can be read as forms of personal names hitherto encountered only or chiefly in the Bible: Adam, Eve, Jabal, Noah, Hagar, Bilhah, Michael, Israel (although decipherment will have to be debated by specialists in cuneiform transcription). *Second,* words that appear infrequently in Hebrew — there are some 1700 words that occur only once in the Hebrew written before A.D. 70 — are attested in Eblaite, often with meanings that cast new light on biblical passages. We must remember that poetry, including Hebrew poetry, often preserves ancient vocabulary and syntax, so that documents in a related Semitic language, even if written 1000 or 1500 years before the biblical text, can be informative about linguistic phenomena that were forgotten in a later period. Much less certain is the import of the Ebla discovery for the dating of the patriarchs (based on a partial misunderstanding that the kings and/or kingdoms of Genesis 14, an Abraham story, were mentioned therein) as well as the claimed Ebla reference to a form of the divine name of the God of Israel, Yahweh (so that there would have been a pre-Israelite Semitic deity named Ya).

---

[4]Articles have appeared in BA almost every year from 1976 through 1981, some of them polemical. Overall, one may compare P. Matthiae, *Ebla: An Empire Rediscovered* (Garden City, NY: Doubleday, 1981) with G. Pettinato, *The Archives of Ebla: An Empire Inscribed in Clay* (Garden City, NY: Doubleday, 1981).

UGARIT

On the Mediterranean coast some 75 miles west-southwest of Ebla lies Ugarit (modern Ras Shamra), excavated by a French expedition in over 30 campaigns since 1929, principally under the leadership of Claude Schaeffer. Although settlement at Ugarit goes back to the seventh millennium B.C., the flourishing period was in the Middle Bronze and Later Bronze period from 2000 to 1200 B.C., when Ugarit was in diplomatic relations with world powers like the Hittites, the Egyptians, the Mitanni, and the Mycenaeans. Ultimately, Ugarit fell to invaders from the Mediterranean, "Sea Peoples" related to the biblical Philistines.

The main importance of the site for biblical studies lies in another immense find of clay cuneiform tablets, some of them in Akkadian (the international language), some of them in a northwestern Semitic language, related to Canaanite and an ancester of Phoenician, henceforth dubbed Ugaritic. Written in an alphabetic system, the main body of Ugaritic tablets stems from the 1400s and 1300s, a period 1000 years later than the Eblaite tablets, but still anterior to the written Bible.

More literary than what has been found in the Eblaite tablets, Ugaritic writings preserve ancient Canaanite myths[5] about the supreme father god El, and the younger more active Baal who slew the sea god Yamm, as well as a sea monster Lotan. (Hitherto the underlying myth was known in the Mesopotamian form where the god Marduk slew Tiamat.) Parallels to Hebrew Elohim and Yahweh have been claimed, especially since in some biblical poems God slays the sea monster Rahab or Leviathan (=Lotan). Examples are found in Isa 27:1; 51:9; Ps 74:13-14; 89:10; and Job

[5]M. D. Coogan, *Stories from Ancient Canaan* (Philadelphia: Westminster, 1978).

26:12. In another legend (Aqhat) there figures Danel, possibly equivalent to the Danel (Daniel) of Ezek 14:14,20 who is associated with such primeval figures as Noah and Job. Even richer for biblical purposes than the religious symbolism of the Ugaritic writings is the variety of poetic format and the wealth of vocabulary and syntactical construction, throwing light on Hebrew poetry. One scholar, the late Mitchell Dahood, composed a three-volume commentary on the Psalms[6] wherein he retranslates many of the obscure verses in the light of Ugaritic parallels and gives them almost entirely new meanings. (It is no accident that Dahood was in the forefront of using Eblaite to throw light on Hebrew poetry also.[7]) The extent to which this is a valid procedure is disputed, but few will deny that the discovery of Ugaritic has proved an important background for the understanding of ancient Hebrew.

MARI

Let us turn our attention next to Mesopotamia, the land of the Euphrates and Tigris rivers, some 300 to 500 miles east from the Mediterranean, where the discovery of ancient documents has thrown light not so much on biblical Hebrew as on early biblical customs. One of the important sites is ancient Mari[8] (Tell Hariri) on the Euphrates, dominating ancient caravan routes to the sea and to the northern river tributaries. Mari was excavated by another French scholar,

---

[6]Anchor Bible volumes 16, 17, 17A (Garden City, NY: Doubleday, 1966-1970). For the applicability of Ugaritic to the Bible, see H. L. Ginsberg in BA 8 (1945) 41-58; reprinted in BAR 2. 34-50; for Ugaritic life and culture, see A. F. Rainey in BA 28 (1965) 102-25; reprinted in BAR 3. 76-99.

[7]Dahood has an "Afterword" in the Pettinato volume (note 4 above), entitled "Ebla, Ugarit, and the Bible."

[8]G. E. Mendenhall in BA 11 (1948) 1-19; reprinted BAR 2. 3-20.

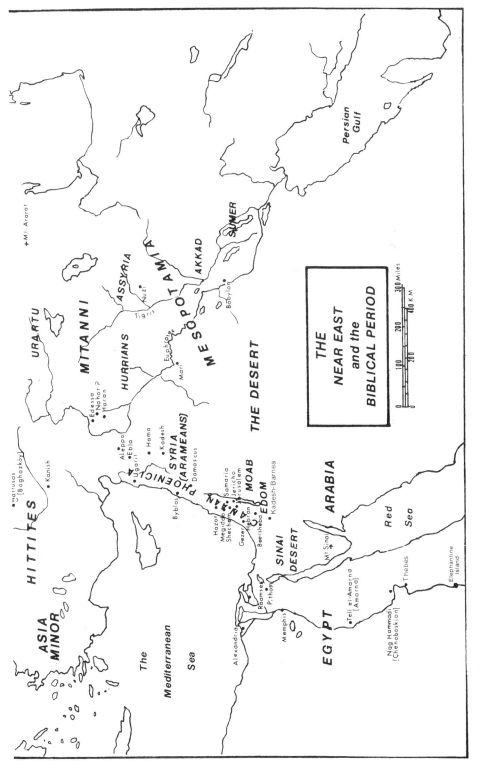

André Parrot, in the period of the 1930s and 1950s. Although settlement there goes back at least to the third millennium (contemporary with Ebla), the chief period of interest for our survey is the *floruit* of 1750-1697 B.C.

Then King Zimri-Lim of Mari was a contemporary and, for a while, an ally of the illustrious Hammurabi of Babylon. The biblical patriarchs are often thought to have lived in the same period; and before the migration of Abraham to Canaan (subsequently "Palestine"), he and his ancestors were located in the region of Haran, an area at times under Mari domination. The Mari site yielded not only a magnificent temple and palace, a ziggurat (step-temple), statues, and paintings, but more importantly 20,000 clay tablets of royal and business archives. Despite the dominant use in these tablets of Akkadian (East Semitic), the majority of the population seems to have been Amorite, a West Semitic people (footnote 3 above) who overran and dominated Mesopotamia by the 18th century, becoming heirs of the great kingdoms of the third millennium. Abraham and his ancestors have sometimes been identified as Amorites; and in the Mari tablets the city Nahor appears, a name borne by Abraham's grandfather (Gen 11:22-25) and by Abraham's brother (11:27-29). Zimri-Lim is described as struggling with the warriors of the Banu-Yamina, "Sons of the Right," a group bearing the same name as one of the subsequent tribes of Israel, Benjamin, also noted for military skills. The curious designation of the Shechemites who dealt with Jacob as the "Sons of the Ass [Hamor]," (Josh 24:32) may reflect the custom attested at Mari of killing an ass to seal an alliance. Indeed, one may wonder if Mari does not supply us with the example of a site where the great myths of the Sumerians and Babylonians were translated into West Semitic languages and underwent local variations. We may have here traces of the path from the great cultures of third-millennium Mesopotamia to the creation and flood narratives of the early chapters of Genesis.

NUZI (NUZU)

Further east, near the Tigris, lay ancient Nuzi or Nuzu (Yoghlan Tepe or Yorghan Tepe), excavated in the late 1920s by an American expedition. Once again the chief biblical interest comes from the find of 5000 cuneiform tablets written in Akkadian even though the population was of another stock. This time non-Semitic Hurrians were involved (biblical Horites and Hivites); for Nuzi lay in a province of the Mitanni Empire, dominated by an Indo-European aristocracy — an empire that in the 1500s and 1400s rivaled Egypt. The patriarchal ancestral region, Haran, was thickly populated by Hurrians and was a Mitanni center. Although the Nuzi tablets date from several hundred years after the Mari tablets, they also enlighten the patriarchal practices,[9] even if the first scholarly claims about "parallels" were a bit overstated. At Nuzi images of the household gods were important symbols of family unity and were generally passed on to the principal heir. The importance of such symbols makes intelligible Rachel's attempt to appropriate the household gods of her father Laban (Gen 31:19,30). It was customary for childless people at Nuzi to adopt someone as son to serve them as long as they lived and to bury them after death; but it was understood that if eventually they had a natural child, this child would become the heir. We find the same situation in Abraham's adopting the slave Eliezer as heir (Gen 15:2-3), only to have him replaced later on by the natural sons Isaac and Ishmael. A wealthy Nuzi wife who did not bear a child was expected to supply the husband with a slave concubine whose children would be counted as the wife's (see Gen

[9]C. H. Gordon in BA 3 (1940); reprinted in BAR 2. 21-33; but see B. L. Eichler in the *Supplementary Volume* to the *Interpreter's Dictionary* 635-36.

A Nuzi Tablet

"Once again the chief biblical interest comes from the
find of 5000 cuneiform tablets written in Akkadian..."

16:2). Deathbed assignments of patrimony at Nuzi when the
parent had "grown old" resemble the opening formula of the
story of the struggle of Jacob and Esau for the birthright:
"When Isaac was old..." (Gen 27:1). These are but a few
examples of how the tablet discoveries of Mesopotamia cast
light on the biblical story. They also create some problems
for dating the patriarchs, but that will be discussed later
(below, p. 75).

HITTITE ARCHIVES

When we move northwest from Mesopotamia, passing
beyond the Mitanni/Hurrian regions, we come to another

formidable empire, ruled by the Hittites with its capital at Ḫattusas (Boghazköy) in eastern Asia Minor. Neither Semite nor Indo-European in their distant origins (third millennium), the Hittites expanded their rule in the second millennium, sacking Babylon (1500s), crushing the Mitanni (1300s), and challenging Egypt and the formidable Pharaoh Ramses II at Kadesh (1285) — only to have their own empire fall victim to invasions by the Sea Peoples and others *ca.* 1200.

The interpretation of cuneiform tablets in imperial Hittite (an Indo-European dialect) was begun in 1915 by B. Hrozný, a Czech scholar, and has now reached a satisfactory level, as has also our knowledge of another Hittite, Indo-European dialect written in hieroglyphics. The biblical "Hittites" (Neo-Hittites) are the mixed heirs of the old Hittite realms, especially Syria. They figure in the patriarchal story (Gen 23:10), and intermarriage with Hittite women was evidently a major issue (Gen 26:34; 27:46). Bathsheba was the wife of Uriah the Hittite when David took advantage of her. Ezekiel (16:3,45) traces Jerusalem to combined Hittite and Amorite origin. However, we must be cautious, for Israelite memory may have confused Hittites and Horites/Hivites (Hurrians).

A major contribution of the Hittite archives to biblical knowledge involves the pattern of suzerainty treaties whereby the Hittite "Great King" made a pact with vassal kingdoms in his sphere of influence. (Such treaties were not unique to the Hittites, but their archives have made available the best examples.) There are resemblances in format and wording to the covenant between God and Israel described in Exodus 20 and Joshua 24.[10] The Hittite king

---

[10]On covenant forms, see G. E. Mendenhall in BA 17 (1954) 50-76; reprinted in BAR 3. 25-53; also D. J. McCarthy, *Old Testament Covenant: A Survey of Current Opinions* (Richmond: Knox, 1972); *Treaty and Covenant* (rev. ed.; Rome: Biblical Institute, 1978).

ORIGINAL PICTOGRAPH	PICTOGRAPH IN POSITION OF LATER CUNEIFORM	EARLY BABYLONIAN	ASSYRIAN	ORIGINAL OR DERIVED MEANING
				BIRD
				FISH
				DONKEY
				OX
				SUN DAY
				GRAIN
				ORCHARD
				TO PLOW TO TILL
				BOOMERANG TO THROW
				TO STAND TO GO

Table showing the development of cuneiform script from pictographs to Assyrian characters. The word cuneiform derives from Latin and means "wedge-shaped." It has been the modern designation from the early 18th century onward for the most widespread and historically significant writing system in the ancient Near East.

identifies himself in the treaty by name, titles, and attributes, even as the Bible gives the name of "Yahweh, the God of Israel" (Josh 24:2; Exod 20:2). This is followed in most Hittite treaties by a historical prologue where the Hittite king describes what he has previously done for the vassals, a prologue that constitutes implicit assurance of continued patronage. Similarly Josh 24:3-13 describes what God did for Abraham and his descendants till Joshua's time. (Indeed, we may speculate that the covenant prologue and its recitation of history may have given shape to some of the narrative collections of the Pentateuch.) Stipulations follow in the treaty, phrased as apodictic imperatives and indicating the king's expectations of his vassal; e.g., Mursilis II specifies, "Thou shalt seize all captives; thou shalt not leave any behind." The Ten Commandments of Exod 20:3-17 and Deut 5:6-21 (also in a "Thou shalt...shalt not" pattern) constitute the stipulations of the covenant between Yahweh and Israel. Sometimes, either explicitly or implicitly, there is a provision for the preservation of the treaty, just as Josh 24:26 mentions the writing of a law book. In fact, the Ark of the Covenant became the repository of the Decalogue for Israel (Deut 31:26). Witnesses to the treaty are listed, even as Josh 24:22,27 appeals to witnesses. Curses are leveled in case the vassal should break the treaty, and a blessing is promised if he keeps it — a pattern well attested in the Bible (Deut 27-28; Josh 8:34). No one imagines that the Bible copied a specific Hittite treaty, but these archives exemplify for us the legal format in which the Israelites would have conceived their special relationship or covenant with God.

AMARNA EGYPTIAN ARCHIVES

The Hittite archives came from a site some 750 miles north of Canaan; the archives of an Egyptian site about the same distance to the southwest of Canaan are equally informative. Amarna (sometimes Tell el-Amarna) is the modern name of ancient Akhtaton, on the Nile roughly half way between Thebes and Memphis. In the period 1375-1350 this city served as the capital for the Pharaoh Amenophis IV or Akhenaton, romantically dubbed the heretic pharaoh because he shifted the focus of Egyptian religion from Amon worshipped at Thebes to the god Aton, the sun disk, for whom he built a new city. It is debatable whether this worship was monotheism, but certainly the Egyptian hymn to Aton has parallels to Psalm 104. The religious reform was accompanied by a new realism in art (the bust of Akhenaton's wife Nefertiti is one of the most beautiful art pieces of antiquity) and by many social changes.

However, the negative aspect of the turmoil produced by Akhenaton is apparent in tablets discovered at Amarna in the last century and published in the first two-thirds of this century.[11] Written in cuneiform Akkadian, they constitute some 375 items from the archives of the Egyptian kings who reigned at this site — correspondence with other kings, but in particular a large number of letters *from* vassal rulers in Palestine and Syria. These latter attest to the decline of Egyptian control, not only because of international rivalry between Egypt and the Mitanni or Hittite Empires, but also because of the incursion of peoples seeking to settle in more civilized regions. In over fifty letters from Byblos to the Egyptian court the peril from an Amorite leader is emphasized. Even more interesting are the constant references to the Hapiru (Habiru or 'Apiru), seemingly a mixture of unlanded vagrants, run-away slaves, and ill-paid mercenaries, who are invading the Canaan area, especially around Shechem. The similarity of this name to "Hebrew" has

---

[11]E. F. Campbell in BA 23 (1960) 2-22; reprinted in BAR 3. 54-75.

raised the possibility that this correspondence in the early 14th century is describing *a phase* of the entrance of Hebrews into Palestine.[12] In the correspondence, the vassal kings of the city-states of Canaan and Syria protest their "loyalty" to the Egyptian pharaoh and ask for protection; but it is quite clear that the monarch can do little. The return of the Egyptian seat of government to Thebes in or before the reign of Akhenaton's son-in-law, Tutankhamon (*ca.* 1350 — the "Tut" of the famous tomb) marked the triumph of realism over romanticism, as Egypt began to seek to restore political order throughout its sphere of influence.

PALESTINIAN FINDS

The tablet or documentary discoveries discussed thus far have all been from outside the main territory of the Old Testament story, namely, that tiny geographical area at the east end of the Mediterranean called Canaan, or Palestine, or Israel. The finds have also been anterior to the main era of Old Testament history which runs from the appearance of the tribes in Palestine (scarcely much after 1200) to the fall of the Judean monarchy (500s). Alas, when one turns to that main Old Testament territory and era, major documentary finds are not forthcoming. We may list some important but minor finds: a potsherd (ostracon) with an early example of the alphabet (from Izbet Sartah [Ebenezer?], *ca.* 1200 B.C.); a pendant with a poetic agricultural calendar (Gezer, *ca.* 900); a basalt stele of Mesha, King of Moab, describing his defeat of Israel (Transjordan, *ca.* 840); twelve Aramaic fragments of wall plaster from the 700s or early 600s at Deir

[12]References to Ḥabiru are found in the Nuzi tablets as well, indicating a wide geographical presence; at most the biblical Hebrews would have been part of a much larger movement.

Cast of Basalt Stele of Mesha,
King of Moab

This stele, the original of which is in the Musee du
Louvre, Paris, describes Mesha's defeat of Israel (Transjordan, *ca.* 840).

'Alla (Succoth?) in the Jordan valley, mentioning Balaam (Numbers 22-24); tax receipts inscribed in ink on potsherds from the capital of Israel during the reign of Jeroboam II (Samaria, *ca.* 750?);[13] an inscription on the wall of the Siloam water passage, describing the tunneling process (Jerusalem, *ca.* 700); some 20 jar fragments inscribed in ink, describing a foreign invasion, perhaps that of Nebuchadnezzar against Jerusalem (Lachish, *ca.* 590?); some 200 ostraca inscribed in Hebrew and in Aramaic (Arad, 600s to 400s).

Illuminating the post-monarchical period of the Old Testament is an important find (early 1960s) of Aramaic fragments, called the Samaria Papyri.[14] References to Persian Emperors date them to 375-335 B.C.; they were brought to a cave in the Wadi Daliyeh (nine miles north of Jericho on the Jordan) by refugees from Samaria, fleeing before Alexander the Great's destruction of the city in 332. These papyri help to fill in the biblical information about the names of the governors of Samaria and of the Jerusalem high priests.

ELEPHANTINE

A more important Aramaic papyri cache pertinent to the early post-monarchical period comes from Egypt. On Elephantine Island in the Nile (opposite Aswan, 100 miles south of Thebes) there was a colony of Hebrews (not necessarily Jews, i..e, of the tribe of Judah). The origin of this colony probably antedated the Persian invasion of Egypt (525), and it was terminated *ca.* 399 B.C. The papyri, found at the end of the 19th century and published in different lots throughout two-thirds of the 20th century, are largely legal

[13] I. T. Kaufman in BA 45 (1982) 229-39.
[14] F. M. Cross in BA 26 (1963) 110-21; reprinted in BAR 3. 227-39.

texts and contracts, reflecting the history of several island families.[15] But there are also letters which reflect on the biblical history. These Hebrews had a temple to the God YHW (Yahu/Yaho) which was destroyed in 410 at the instigation of hostile Egyptian priests. Consequently, the Elephantine Hebrews wrote to Bagoas, governor of Judea, asking him for intercessory help. The names of Sanballat and of the high priest Johanan appear in this correspondence, throwing light on information in Neh 12:22 and on the dating of biblical Ezra. These names, when combined with those found in the Samaria papyri, give us a sequence of Judean notables in the 400s and 300s. Evidently the request for help was successful and the temple rebuilt for at least a short period. Religion at Elephantine, practiced far from Jerusalem and the main Jewish centers, seems to have undergone considerable outside influence, even to the point of positing a female consort for YHW.

DEAD SEA SCROLLS

Let us move ahead chronologically to the Judaism of the period just before the birth of Jesus. Almost by way of compensation for its previous failure to supply documentary finds, Palestine offers us perhaps the greatest single biblical cache of all time. For a decade beginning in 1947, in caves on the west side of the Dead Sea, Bedouin discovered scrolls and fragments of some 600 manuscripts.[16] The prin-

---

[15]E. G. Kraeling in BA 15 (1952) 50-67; reprinted in BAR 1. 128-44; also B. Porten 42 (1979) 74-104 (technical, after initial pages).

[16]For overall analysis see F. M. Cross, *The Ancient Library of Qumran* (2 ed.; Garden City, NY: Doubleday, 1961); best translation by G. Vermes, *The Dead Sea Scrolls in English* (2 ed.; New York: Penguin, 1975); good survey by J. A. Sanders in BA 36 (1973) 110-48. For the

cipal finds were in eleven caves near a site called Qumran, ten miles south of Jericho. Excavations of the site by R. de Vaux and G. L. Harding between 1951 and 1956 uncovered a set of community buildings (water system, kitchen, dining rooms, pantries, pottery workshops, scriptorium) which were occupied from *ca.* 135 B.C. to *ca.* 31 B.C., and in a second period from *ca.* A.D. 1 to 68. This agrees with the paleographic evidence dating most of the scrolls and fragments to the last two centuries B.C. and to the first century A.D.

It is now generally agreed that at Qumran have been discovered the central settlement and the libraries of the Essenes, one of the three sects of the Jews by Josephus' reckoning (*Antiquities* 13.5.9 #171) whose city in the desert is described by Pliny the Elder (*Natural History* 5.17.73) as situated on the west shore of the Dead Sea, north of En Gedi. The Essenes, like the other two sects (Pharisees and Sadducees), were the offshoot of the Jewish revolt against Syrian dominance, a revolt which began under the leadership of the Maccabees in 167 B.C. against the hated Antiochus IV Epiphanes who had plundered the Temple and set up an altar to the Olympian Zeus. Eventually, *ca.* 152 Jonathan, brother of Judas Maccabeus, appropriated the high priesthood in which office he was followed by his brother Simon (143), thus establishing the Hasmonean dynasty. The Essenes seem to have been ultra-pious Jews who protested the Maccabean usurpation of the high priesthood, insisting on a purer Zadokite lineage, and who withdrew to the Dead Sea area to separate themselves from the profanation of Jerusalem. Perhaps they were fueled numerically

recently published Temple Scroll, see J. Milgrom in BA 41 (1978) 105-20. Another important Dead Sea find was at Murabba'at, 12 miles south of Qumran, pertinent to Bar Kokhba's revolt in A.D. 132-135; see articles by Y. Yadin in BA 24 (1961) 34-50, 86-95; reprinted in BAR 3. 254-78.

and theologically in their protest by Jews returning from Babylon who disagreed with Maccabean/Hasmonean religious innovation.[17] The Essene settlement at Qumran was interrupted for part of the reign of Herod the Great (37-4 B.C.); an earthquake was the immediate cause but the suspicions of Herod may have contributed. Resettled, the site was destroyed by Roman armies in A.D. 68 as part of the First Jewish War.

The biblical interest of the Qumran or Dead Sea manuscripts is manifold. *First*, of the biblical books in the Hebrew canon (footnote 2 above), all but Esther are found at Qumran. As we shall see below, hitherto our oldest complete Hebrew text of the Old Testament dated from the tenth century A.D. Now from Qumran there come, at times, whole scrolls of biblical books 1000 years earlier.[18] The Hebrew biblical text at Qumran is not necessarily better than the standard Hebrew text already known (although in some cases it is, e.g., Books of Samuel); but the diversity of the textual traditions now available helps to fill in our knowledge of how biblical books were copied and preserved. Some of the Hebrew fragments agree not with the standard Hebrew Bible but with the Greek translation (Septuagint) or with the Samaritan Pentateuch. In other words, for much of the Bible, Qumran antedates the standardization process effected by the rabbis in the second century.

Second, deuterocanonical books (footnote 2) have been largely preserved in Greek; now Qumran has yielded some of the Aramaic original of Tobit and the Hebrew Sirach.

Third, targums or translations of the Hebrew biblical books into Aramaic (the spoken language of many Jews) were known to us previously from the second century A.D.

[17]J. Murphy-O'Connor in BA 40 (1977) 100-24.
[18]See P. W. Skehan in BA 28 (1965) 87-100; reprinted in BAR 3. 240-53.

and later. Qumran supplies considerably earlier evidence, e.g., a *Targum of Job* from Cave 11 which may have been composed in the second century B.C. Targums are important for textual study, as a way of reconstructing the Hebrew text that underlies the Aramaic translation. They also enlighten the history of theology, since the translation betrays how a passage was understood at this early period.

Fourth, many manuscripts of well-known apocryphal books of pre-Christian Judaism (*Enoch, Jubilees*, some Patriarchal *Testaments*) have turned up in their original Aramaic or Hebrew. Hitherto we had been dependent on translations of translations, e.g., Ethiopic from Greek. These works are extremely important for reconstructing the variety of theological thought in intertestamental Judaism — a Judaism upon which Christianity drew.

Fifth, a considerable body of Qumran literature consists of documents composed by the Essenes themselves: several editions of their rule of life; commentaries on the biblical prophets who, they thought, were writing about them and their history; hymns; visions of God's future plans, whether those involved a war between light and darkness or the perfect temple and state. Relatively little "second-Temple" (pre-70 A.D.) Pharisee thought has been preserved, and virtually nothing of Sadducee origin, so that the Qumran discovery of Essene literature is a major contribution to our knowledge of Judaism.

But it is also significant for Christianity since the Essenes and the early Jewish Christians had many common features. Both strongly emphasized the coming of the Messiah and the fulfillment of God's plans, along with the need to reform a nucleus of Israel for that moment. (An obvious difference is that one group thought that the Messiah would come soon; the other group thought that he had already come.) Among common features shared by Essene and Christian theology and community life we may list the following: a basic appeal to Isa 40:3, "Prepare the way of the Lord... in the desert"; a firm sense of community and oneness, including some community of goods; entrance to the community on Pentecost; initiatory washing connected to the outpouring of the Spirit; a sacred meal of bread and wine; eschatological stress on celibacy; rejection of divorce; a dualistic view of humanity, divided into children of light and of darkness, children of truth and of falsehood (a view especially common in I John); an important place allotted to the Spirit of Truth; a special symbolism for Melchizedek; a community role given to a group of twelve; a supervisor (overseer, bishop) who cared for the common goods and inspected the doctrine of members, serving as a shepherd to his people; meetings of the members called "the Many" (see Acts 6:5; 15:12). The Qumran hymns and the hymns in Luke 1-2 (Magnificat, Benedictus, Gloria, Nunc Dimittis) have many similarities both in format and in the technique of rephrasing Old Testament passages. While there is no evidence of Qumran knowledge of Christians or of direct Christian dependence upon existing Qumran literature, the Dead Sea Scrolls offer important information about how Christianity may have developed from intertestamental Judaism and about the Palestinian thought-world in which Jesus lived.

NAG HAMMADI (CHENOBOSKION)

Another find of manuscripts hidden in jars was made in Egypt at almost the same time (1945) as the Dead Sea discovery in Palestine. This time 13 codices or books (with 1240 inscribed pages) were involved rather than scrolls, and the language was Coptic (a language descended from ancient Egyptian but heavily influenced by Greek).[19] The site is near the town of Nag Hammadi, on the bend of the Nile some 75 miles north of Thebes; and in the fourth century A.D. the area was dotted with Christian monasteries. Chenoboskion (Chenoboskeia), where the great St. Pachomius (292-346) was converted and began his life as a hermit, was one of these; and the codices surely came from the library of such a monastery.

There are 46 works (plus 6 duplicates, making 52 tractates in all), and 40 of them are nowhere else preserved. While the translation into Coptic took place at different times and in different regions (as we can tell from the dialects), the works were originally in Greek. There is all the variety of a library: Plato's *Republic*, non-Christian writing on Seth, Jewish works, and Christian compositions from the second to fourth centuries representing different theological views. What seems to unite such writing is that all these works could be read as giving special knowledge (Greek *gnōsis*) to those who know what to look for. Pachomius himself was an orthodox Christian, but there is evidence that gnosticism infiltrated Egyptian monasteries,[20] and we know of anti-heretical purges that took place under the influence of Epiphanius and of Athanasius (the famous fourth-century bishop of Alexandria). It may have been in fear of such a purge that the collection was buried for safekeeping or for posterity.

[19]See BA 42 (1979) 206-56 (whole issue). For the texts: J. M. Robinson, *The Nag Hammadi Library in English* (San Francisco: Harper & Row, 1977).

[20]Christian gnosticism is not easy to define, since the Church Fathers of Alexandria (e.g., Clement) had strains of gnosticism that were not frowned upon as heterodox. Those gnostics ultimately deemed heretical were not of one mind among themselves. Prominent in one system or the

A few of the Christian works may contain authentic memories of Jesus not preserved in the canonical New Testament. The chief candidate for such preservation is *The Gospel of Thomas*, where occasionally there are sayings of Jesus in a more primitive form than that attested in the Synoptic Gospels. However, for the most part, the importance of the library is for church history, augmenting our knowledge of how Christian gnostics of the second and third centuries thought and wrote, as distinct from a mirror image gained from what the Church Fathers wrote about them (especially Irenaeus and Epiphanius).[21] In a sense, then, the discovery might seem to lie beyond the biblical area that is the focus of this book. However, certain strains of protognostic thought appear in the New Testament, and we may be finding in the Nag Hammadi treatises more developed forms of New Testament gnosticism. Already I Timothy 6:20 warns, "Avoid the godless chatter and contradictions of what is falsely called *gnōsis*." I John 4:2 and II John 7 stress the importance of believing in Jesus Christ as one come "in the flesh." A full-scale denial of the fleshly reality of the crucified Jesus is found in several of the Nag Hammadi treatises. For instance, in *The Apocalypse of Peter* the crucifiers are torturing only the substitute fleshly Jesus, while the living Jesus stands off laughing at the whole process. II Timothy 2:18 attacks those who hold that the

---

other were such ideas as: a series of eons separating the Unknowable God from creation; the creator god of the Old Testament was evil or a demigod because he brought matter into existence; pre-existent souls were entrapped in this matter; Jesus entered the world (even if he never really became part of it) in order to reveal to such souls their origin; such revealed knowledge (*gnōsis*) enables souls to escape the entrapment of matter.

[21] For the subtleties of the issue, see Pheme Perkins, *The Gnostic Dialogue: The Early Church and the Crisis of Gnosticism* (New York: Paulist, 1980).

resurrection of Christians has already taken place. The late second-century Nag Hammadi *Treatise on Resurrection* assures the addressee (Rheginos), "You already have resurrection." Titus 1:9 and Acts 20:28-30 give the presbyter-bishops of the Church the task of refuting the false teachers. A reaction from the other side may be heard in the hostility of *The Apocalypse of Peter* against "Those outside our number who name themselves bishop and also deacons, as if they have received authority from God." It is very clear that each side is charging the other with heresy and error. And if in II Peter 1:20; 3:2,15-17, Peter becomes spokesman of apostolic authority guiding the faithful, in *The Gospel of Mary* (a work related to the Nag Hammadi find) Mary Magdalene is held up as the disciple whom Jesus loved more than he loved Peter and the others. She proclaims special revelation, disturbing Peter and Andrew for whom her teachings are "strange ideas."

Thus we learn from the discovery of gnostic writings how complex the intra-Christian battles were. The late second-century *Adversus Haereses* of Irenaeus clearly diagnosed the gnostics as unorthodox; and having read the abstruse reflections in the Nag Hammadi treatises, we agree that gnostic views had traveled an enormous distance from Jesus of Nazareth. But these documents also make us realize that the decisions about orthodoxy and heterodoxy were easier in retrospect than in the heart of the conflict, and that the opponents on each side had their own integrity. Irenaeus and the writers of the Nag Hammadi codices were by no means equally valuable for Christianity or equally faithful to the New Testament; but both would have to be judged equally passionate in their devotion to what they regarded as truth.

COPIES OF THE BIBLE

Besides documentary finds that cast light on the Bible, some discoveries (or re-discoveries) have increased our knowledge of how the Scriptures were preserved. The Hebrew Bible most used by students in modern times[22] was largely based on a vocalized text copied in A.D. 1008, known as the Leningrad Codex. A note at the end of this codex associates it with the tradition of the Ben Asher family which lived at Tiberias in Galilee in the tenth century. An earlier copy of the Hebrew Scriptures by Aaron ben Asher, dated to about 930, had been kept by the Karaites (a Jewish sect) in Jerusalem. It was seen at Cairo by the great Maimonides who maintained that it should serve as a model for copying scrolls of the Law. By the Middle Ages its presence was attested in Aleppo, whence the name Aleppo Codex; and in modern times it was thought to have been destroyed there during anti-Jewish riots in 1947. However, 600 of the 800 pages were preserved and smuggled into Israel in 1956. Now at last this superior manuscript, the oldest codex of the entire Hebrew Bible, has been published and can serve critical scholarship.[23]

Paradoxically, the Old Testament in Greek (Septuagint) has been preserved for us in earlier copies than the Old Testament in Hebrew. One of the oldest copies of the Septuagint is the fourth-century A.D. Codex Sinaiticus, part of which was discovered at St. Catherine's Monastery in the Sinai desert in the middle of the last century by Konstantin von Tischendorf. From a total of approximately 730 leaves some 476 have been kept in London (British Museum) and some 43 in Leipzig. The rest was thought to be lost, until in

[22]R. Kittel and P. Kahle, *Biblia hebraica* (3 ed.; Stuttgart: Wurtemburg. Bibelanstalt, 1937).
[23]M. Goshen-Gottstein guided the publication by the Hebrew University Bible Project; see BA 42 (1979) 145-63.

14th verse of I John in Codex Sinaiticus

"One of the oldest copies of the Septuagint is the fourth-century A.D. Codex Sinaiticus, part of which was discovered at St. Catherine's Monastery in the middle of the Sinai desert..."

1975, in clearing debris beneath a church at the monastery, the monks found an old cell which contained manuscripts buried hundreds of years ago, perhaps by a collapsed ceiling. They are in several languages; but those in Greek are frequently in the uncial or capital letters characteristic of the most ancient Christian copyists. There seem to be 10 complete codices and parts of what could be more. Some 8 to 14 leaves of Codex Sinaiticus are in the find. Publication is eagerly awaited.[24]

The great fourth- and fifth-century codices of the Bible were copied on vellum or skin. Fragments of even earlier copies of New Testament books on papyrus, mostly from Egypt, have been discovered in this century. In 1935 a fragment of The Gospel of John, postage-stamp in size and known as the Rylands Papyrus (P[52]), was published; it was written about A.D. 135 and is very important for the dating of John. Another mid-second-century set of fragments (Papyrus Egerton 2), published in 1935, contains gospel passages resembling a mixture from the various canonical Gospels. A few scholars contend that this work is independent of the four Gospels preserved in the New Testament, but most think of it as a compilation. In the 1950s and 1960s the Bodmer collection of early papyri was published.[25] It contained lengthy late-second-century copies of John (P[66]) and of Luke/John (P[75]). The latter agrees closely with Codex Vaticanus copied almost two centuries later, an agreement illustrating the fidelity of the scribes. The former papyrus has a somewhat different textual tradition from Vaticanus, closer at times to Codex Sinaiticus; this diversity shows that the different textual traditions of the later period already existed in the early centuries. In our modern libraries books printed in the last century are crumbling to dust; it is humbling to think that the dryness of the Judean desert near the Dead Sea and of the Egyptian desert near the Nile have preserved such papyri for almost 2000 years.

[24]J. H. Charlesworth in BA 42 (1979) 174-79; 43 (1980) 26-34; it is difficult to get clear information about what has been found. See also P. Mayerson in BA 46 (1983) 54-56 on where Codex Sinaiticus was written.
[25]F. V. Filson in BA 22 (1959) 48-51; 25 (1962) 50-57; both reprinted in BAR 3. 304-14.

DUBIOUS FINDS

The documentary discoveries listed above explain some of the excitement prevalent in modern biblical studies. But it may be wise to close this section of the book by some cautions about the care to be exercised in judging new "discoveries." If the west side of the Dead Sea has yielded remarkable scrolls in the middle of this century, a major find from the east side of that sea was reported already in 1883. M. W. Shapira, a Jerusalem antiquities dealer, tried to sell to the British Museum 15 strips of parchment containing an early Hebrew text of Deuteronomy discovered in the Dead Sea area. However, the careful investigation by Clermont-Ganneau and others suggested that the strips were a forgery. A modern attempt to prove them genuine in the light of the Dead Sea Scrolls has had little success.[26]

On the other side of the world at almost the same time another "discovery" was being made. In 1874 L. Neto, Director of the National Museum in Rio de Janeiro, announced that he had received a copy of what was alleged to be a Phoenician inscription carved in stone, discovered in northeastern Brazil. The text related how a group of Phoenician ships was blown off course to Brazil. Once again careful scholarship suggested a forgery; and a modern attempt to prove genuineness has had little following.[27]

In the early 1970s a Spanish Jesuit working in Rome, José O'Callaghan, thought that he detected a few letters of a passage from Mark's Gospel on fragments in Greek from Cave 7 of Qumran. This identification implied a very early date for Mark (40s) and a knowledge of Christianity by the

---

[26]See "The Shapira Affair" in BARev 5 (#4, 1979) 12-27.
[27]F. M. Cross in BARev 5 (#1, 1979) 36-43.

Dead Sea Essenes. However, the identification has been rejected by the majority of those who studied the evidence.[28] Such scholarly vigilance is reassuring to those who may wonder about the scientific quality of Bible study.

[28]For the basic fragments see the Supplement to the *Journal of Biblical Literature* 91/92 (1972) 1-20. J. A. Fitzmyer, *The Dead Sea Scrolls* (Bibliography; Missoula: Scholars Press, 1975) 119 comments: "Favorable reactions to the claims have come only from uncritical sources."

PART II

Archaeological Discoveries
and
History

Archaeological Discoveries and History

WHILE DOCUMENTARY finds make the largest head-lines, non-documentary archaeological discoveries may tell even more about life in the biblical period. For instance, defensive walls and gates reveal military strength and the warlike character of the times; palaces reflect wealth, artistic accomplishments, and the ideology and grandeur of the monarchy; temples express religious aspirations and theo-logical insights; streets and homes show the standard of life, how businesses were conducted and households were main-tained. Of course, even if we confine our report to archaeol-ogy in *the Holy Land*, the spectrum of finds goes far beyond the biblical era. At one end it reaches back into the Stone Ages and to the beginnings of agriculture and of cities, as well as to the civilizations in the land before the Israelites came. At the other end of the spectrum Palestinian archaeology uncovers post-biblical cultures, e.g., syn-agogues and cemeteries from the times of the early rabbis, and Christian churches from the times of the early bishops; Arab palaces reflecting the Islamic conquest; magnificent crusader fortresses and churches, succeeded in turn by walls and structures indicative of Turkish supremacy. But in what follows we are concentrating on the relatively short biblical interval (1850 B.C. to A.D. 150) that is a small part of the

10,000 year archaeological record. And even then only a few outstanding sites can be given attention — those that illustrate the clarification and the confusion brought to the Bible by archaeological investigations.

JERICHO

On a plain between the Judean mountains and the Jordan river, next to a spring that attracted settlers, the large tell (a mound raised by levels of settlement) that marks the site of ancient Jericho has been an example of the failures and achievements of Palestinian "digging." The father of Palestinian exploration, Edward Robinson, assumed in 1831 that the mound consisted of accumulated rubbish. The first major excavation, conducted by an Austrian/German expedition in 1907-1909 (E. Sellin, C. Watzinger), represented an early stage in scientific knowledge when no accurate method had been devised for dating the finds.[29] The huge trench that was excavated cut across massive defensive walls, and inevitably the biblical description of the walls of Jericho (Joshua 6) was invoked in discussing these defenses.

In the 1920s and early 1930s the distinguished American biblical-archaeological scholar, W. F. Albright of the Johns Hopkins University, conducted an excavation at Tell Beit Mirsim (biblical Debir?), some 40 miles to the southwest of Jericho, on the other side of the Judean mountains toward the Mediterranean. While this site did not yield startling finds, Albright was able to develop a reasonably accurate Palestinian ceramic chronology. Sites are dotted with the

---

[29]For a perceptive history of the development of archaeological method in Palestine/ Israel, see W. G. Dever BA 43 (1980) 40-48. Also H. D. Lance, *The Old Testament and the Archaeologist* (Philadelphia: Fortress, 1981).

Jericho

A circular tower (bottom left) is part of the Jericho city wall. "Fascinating was the discovery of a huge tower and walls built before the art of pottery had been discovered, and admiration was evoked by the highly artistic plastered skulls and face masks of that supposedly primitive period."

fragments (sherds) of broken pots which often can be assembled into whole artifacts exhibiting diversities in pottery style and shape. When an exemplar of a particular pottery style is found together with a datable object (an inscription, or seal, or cartouche that allows crossdating with known Egyptian or Mesopotamian rulers) *in a sealed context*, so that a later piece could not have become mixed up with an earlier piece, one can gain an idea of when that style of pottery was in vogue. In turn, the pottery can be used to date buildings and walls.

Consequently, when the second major excavation of Jericho was conducted in 1936, this time under British auspices (J. Garstang), the scientific technology had improved. But the mound still proved infuriatingly complicated in terms of stratigraphy. For example, there were 18 detectable layers of settlement, fallen walls lying almost horizontal, and dump pits from previous excavations which were poorly charted. Particular interest centered upon the large fourth city built on the site at a time when Palestine was under Egyptian dominance (Garstang's Layer III). The destruction of the walls of that city by a great conflagration was dated by Garstang to the Late Bronze period (1550-1200), specifically to 1400. Albright disagreed, for he dated the destruction closer to or after 1300.

After the Second War Jericho was excavated once more (1952-1958), this time by Kathleen Kenyon. She had worked in British archaeology with Sir Mortimer Wheeler and had developed an exquisitely minute system for noting stratigraphy.[30] This served her excellently in wrestling with the complicated occupations of Jericho, as did the new radiocarbon method of dating. The site was already occupied in Mesolithic times, 8000 years before Christ, but a major part of the mound consisted of Neolithic strata. Fascinating was

---

[30]K. M. Kenyon, *Digging up Jericho* (London: Praeger, 1957).

the discovery of a huge tower and walls built before the art of pottery had been discovered, and admiration was evoked by the highly artistic plastered skulls and face masks of that supposedly primitive period. Cities rose and fell in the Early Bronze Age (3rd millennium), marked by 17 phases of walls. By Middle Bronze IIA and B (1900-1650) there was a high point in the history of Jericho marked by a new culture resembling that of coastal Syria (Amorite?). In its final Middle Bronze stage, the city was defended by an immense beaten-earth embankment or glacis, often associated with the military architecture of the Hyksos, the foreigners who dominated Egypt from 1730 to 1570. Here was Garstang's fourth city, but the violent destruction of that city clearly had to be dated to about 1560 when the Hyksos were expelled from Egypt — hundreds of years earlier than either Garstang or Albright had thought. Even more puzzling were the very scant signs of settlement during the Late Bronze period. While some allowance must be made for erosion, it seems indisputable that no great city occupied the site at the period (1300s or 1200s) fixed by most scholars for the Israelite invasion of Canaan. If the walls of Jericho came tumbling down, they did so centuries before!

The Bible reports that Jericho was cursed by Joshua (6:26) so that there was seemingly no major reoccupation until that by Hiel in the time of Ahab (I Kings 16:34; *ca.* 850 B.C.). One may guess that such reoccupation was on a small scale and it may have been eroded by time; but, in fact, careful excavation has uncovered no signs of it. Archaeology has been kinder to the New Testament mention of a Jericho visited by Jesus (Mark 10:46-52). About two miles south of the mound of the older Jericho, an American expedition in the 1950s excavated magnificent pools, palaces, baths, and gymnasia, built by the Hasmonean priest-kings and by Herod in the 150 years before Jesus' ministry. Evidently the warm weather of the Jordan valley made Jericho a Herodian winter resort.

HAZOR

Another great excavation marked the period immediately after the Second War, as a new group of scholars entered Palestinian archaeology in force — the Israelis, now exploring the terrain of the new state they had carved out of Palestine. Between 1955 and 1958 and again in 1968 a distinguished Israeli soldier-scholar, Yigael Yadin, excavated the immense mound of Hazor on the west side of the Jordan rift valley, some 8 miles north of the Sea of Galilee.[31] Garstang had done 5 soundings in the mound in 1928 and had dated the final destruction of the site to 1400 B.C. As with Jericho, this dating seemed to fix the Israelite conquest of Canaan, since Josh 11:10-13 described how Joshua burned Hazor, "formerly the head of all these kingdoms." With more accurate methods, Yadin traced settlement at Hazor back to the Early Bronze Age and detected an immense expansion of city dwelling in the Middle Bronze Age — probably the era in which Hazor became the largest city in Canaan. Unlike Jericho, however, Hazor was a city in the Late Bronze Age as well. This city was violently destroyed just before 1200 and the occupation in the following century was of another, less sophisticated type. Surely, the destruction marked the passing of the site into the hands of the Israelite invaders.

An important feature of the pre-Israelite era was a series of super-imposed temples, representing rebuildings from the Middle Bronze into the Late Bronze Age. The architecture of the last Canaanite temple consisted of a porch, a hall, and an inner sanctum. A similar architectural plan has been

[31] Yadin's articles in BA from 1956 through 1959 are gathered in BAR 2. 191-224. Also Y. Yadin, *Hazor* (Schweich Lectures; London: Oxford, 1972).

found in temples in other Canaanite and Syrian sites, and seemingly it inspired the architects of Solomon's Temple with its porch, holy place, and Holy of Holies. [32] A rich find of cultic vessels and of an altar was made in the Hazor temple area; in particular, a large round basalt basin may have been the antecedent of the bronze "sea" of Solomon's Temple (I Kings 7:23-26).

According to I Kings 9:15, Hazor was rebuilt by Solomon (*ca.* 950), along with Megiddo and Gezer; it was conquered two centuries later (732) by the Assyrians. This basic sketch has been confirmed at Hazor by Yadin's excavation. There was a fortified city at Hazor in the tenth century (Stratum X) with gates and a wall structure similar to those found at Megiddo and Gezer; and there was a major destruction of the city at the end of the eighth century (Stratum V). Not mentioned in the Old Testament but apparent in the excavation was the flourishing era of Hazor (Stratum VIII) under the dynasty of Omri and Ahab (875-850), hated in the Bible for their syncretistic religious policies, but among the ablest statesmen in the history of the Israelite monarchy. A large pillared storehouse, attributed wrongly to Solomon by Garstang, belongs to the Omri-Ahab era, as does a citadel and a complicated underground water system. Evidently Hazor had become for these kings an important defensive site against invasion from the east across the Jordan.

Parenthetically, it should be mentioned that at Samaria itself, the capital city built by Omri, earlier excavations in 1908-1910 and 1931-1935 showed the material elegance of the wealthy eighth-century dynasty. [33] (More recent excavations at Samaria in 1965 and 1968 enlightened chiefly the

[32] For collected articles on Ancient Near East Temples, see BA 8 (1944) 41-88; reprinted in BAR 1. 145-200. Also Carol L. Meyers in BA 45 (1982) 33-41.

[33] G. E. Wright in BA 22 (1959) 67-78; reprinted in BAR 2. 248-57.

post-Exilic history of the city.) The buildings at Samaria were among the finest ever constructed in Palestine. Five hundred ivory fragments, mostly inlays from wall paneling, furniture and decorated boxes, illustrate the reference in I Kings 22:39 to the ivory house built by Ahab, and also provide background for Amos' prophetic words (6:1,4) addressed to "Those who feel secure on the mountain of Samaria" when he castigated "All those who lie upon beds of ivory."

MEGIDDO

Canaan or Palestine is divided in two by the great plain of Esdraelon (Jezreel), running NW-SE from the Bay of Haifa to the Jordan valley. To the south of the plain are the mountains of Samaria and Judea; to the north are the mountains of Galilee. On the southern edge of Esdraelon were fortresses controlling passes from the mountains into the plain, passes through which armies had to travel as they moved from south to north, i.e., from Egypt toward Syria and Mesopotamia. One of these fortresses, Megiddo, has seen so many battles that its name has become synonymous with ultimate war: Armageddon (Rev 16:16) reflects the *har* (Hebrew for "mountain") of Megiddo.

Curiously, in the early biblical story of Israel (Josh 12:21; 17:11; 21:25; Judg 1:27; 5:19) Taanach, another of the Esdraelon fortresses, gets as much attention as, or even more than, Megiddo. But in the time of Solomon, Megiddo comes to biblical importance as a storehouse and a center for horses and chariots (I Kings 4:12; 9:15). Kings of Judah, such as Ahaziah in 842 B.C. (II Kings 9:27) and Josiah in 609 (II Kings 23:29-30), came to a bloody death at Megiddo.

Excavations were first done by the Germans (G. Schumacher) in 1903-1905. As at Jericho, a huge trench that was cut through the mound showed many strata of occupation

Remains of the Storehouses at Megiddo
"But in the time of Solomon, Megiddo comes to biblical importance as a storehouse and a center for horses and chariots (1 Kings 4:12; 9:15)."

but offered little by way of exact dating. From 1925 until 1939 the Oriental Institute of Chicago conducted the largest expedition ever seen in Palestine, attempting to peel off the whole mound stratum by stratum. (Fortunately, that task proved too large, for some parts of a mound should be left to be excavated by future generations with an improved technology). Twenty strata of occupation were uncovered reaching back to the Chalcolithic Age in the fourth millennium. Once again there were cities with immense walls in the Early Bronze and in the Middle Bronze Ages, and the latter period was marked by palaces, temples, ivory treasures, and a Hyksos glacis. In the Late Bronze Age (1550-1200) there were more strata of occupation showing Egyptian influence — not surprising since letters from the prince of Megiddo were found in the Amarna archives in Egypt (above. p. 34).

The carved ivories discovered in the last phase of the pre-Israelite era were magnificent, and a massive temple has been uncovered similar to that found in Shechem (see below). There was a major destruction in the thirteenth century, presumably by the Israelites. American excavations under Paul Lapp between 1963 and 1968 at neighboring Taanach show a destruction in 1468 B.C. but no major consequent occupation until after 1300. One wonders, then, why the biblical account of the Israelite wars with the Canaanites seem to feature Taanach more than Megiddo (Josh 12:21).

The greatest problem resulting from the Megiddo excavations in the 1930s[34] centered on remarkable constructions in Stratum IV which were attributed to the time of Solomon (900s) — a city wall, a palace, a city gate, and stables for horses. There were other gates and walls, and so confusion with a later period was possible. Consequently, Yigael Yadin, fresh from the excavation of Hazor (a site mentioned together with Megiddo and Gezer in I Kings 9:15 as the site of Solomonic building), re-excavated Megiddo to straighten out the chronology of the monarchical period.[35] Some of the Solomonic structures (city wall with casemates, and a gate with four chambers) proved to be the work of the Omri-Ahab dynasty, work completed a century after Solomon's time. Water systems thought to be pre-Solomonic were also re-dated with their later stage attributed to the period of Omri. However, a magnificent city gate with six chambers and two towers does belong to Solomon's era as do similar gates at Hazor and Gezer. Like the campaigns at Hazor, the excavations of Megiddo confirm part of the biblical report about Solomon's building activity, but also challenge the Bible's neglect of Omri and Ahab.

---

[34]G. E. Wright in BA 13 (1950) 28-46; reprinted in BAR 2. 225-39.
[35]Y. Yadin in BA 23 (1960) 62-68; reprinted in BAR 2. 240-47.

SHECHEM

South of Megiddo and near Samaria, the capital city of Omri, lies Shechem (adjacent to modern Nablus). This city controlled the pass where the road from Jerusalem to the north had to turn west to pass between the twin Samaritan mountain peaks named Gerizim and Ebal. In the patriarchal narratives of Genesis, Abraham came to Shechem (12:6), as did Jacob (33:18) and Joseph (37:12-14); and the oak or terebinth of Shechem was a place of cult (35:4). Gerizim and Ebal were the sites of covenant promises and curses (Deut 27:12-13); and in the account of Judges 9, Shechem was the site of the first attempt at monarchy in Israel. There Abimelech ruled for 3 years, eventually seeking to eliminate those in the city who resisted his rule. These people of "the Tower of Shechem" took refuge in "the stronghold of the house of El-Berith" (the God of the Covenant). Later when Rehoboam, son of Solomon, went to receive support from the tribes of Israel (as distinct from Judah) he traveled to Shechem (I Kings 12:1). When Jeroboam succeeded in his revolt against Rehoboam (*ca.* 922 B.C.), he made Shechem the first capital of the ten northern tribes (I Kings 12:25).

There had been a German excavation of Shechem (chiefly by E. Sellin) in 1913-1914 and again in 1926-1934, but the stratification of the site was left badly confused. A major American expedition began in 1956 and continued until 1973 (G. E. Wright, E. F. Campbell).[36] Traces of 24 periods of occupation were uncovered. After the oldest finds from the Chalcolithic era in the fourth millennium B.C., the excavation found a gap until occupation in the Middle

---

[36]A series of articles in BA from 1957 through 1963 are gathered in BAR 2. 258-300. See also G. E. Wright, *Shechem: The Biography of a Biblical City* (New York: McGraw Hill, 1965).

Bronze Age (1900-1550). Seemingly the patriarchal visits described in the Bible would have to be localized in the latter era, when Shechem was a well-fortified city containing a sacred fortress-temple. Late Bronze cities began about 1450 B.C. and lasted until a destruction in 1125. In this era the fortress-temple was replaced in the sacred precinct by a massive one-room temple. If one associates the destruction of 1125 B.C. with the Abimelech story of Judges 9, this temple may have been dedicated to El-berith. However, such an identification would mean that there was no destructive break in the Late Bronze period between Canaanite and Israelite occupation. Outside the city, on the flanks of Gerizim, another sanctuary has been discovered, perhaps throwing light on the terebinth cultic place of the patriarchs, and/or on the covenant renewal place noted by Deuteronomy.

Prosperity marked the monarchical period at Shechem when the city was continuously occupied, reflecting the aftermath of King Jeroboam's patronage. This prosperity lasted even when, according to the Bible, the capital was shifted to nearby Samaria by King Omri. Destruction of Shechem by the Assyrians came in 724 B.C. In Hellenistic times a city flourished from 330 to 107 B.C.; for seemingly when Alexander the Great burned Samaria, Shechem became the center of the Samaritan community (Josephus, *Antiquities* 11.8.6; #340).[37] In the early part of this era the Samaritans built a temple to God on a section of Gerizim known today as Tell er-Râs. This temple was destroyed in 128 B.C. by the Jewish High Priest John Hyrcanus who attacked from Jerusalem. Such destruction hardened the already bad relationships between Samaritans and Jews. The temple site would have been in ruins during Jesus'

[37]For Mount Gerizim and the Samaritans, see R. T. Anderson in BA 43 (1980) 217-21.

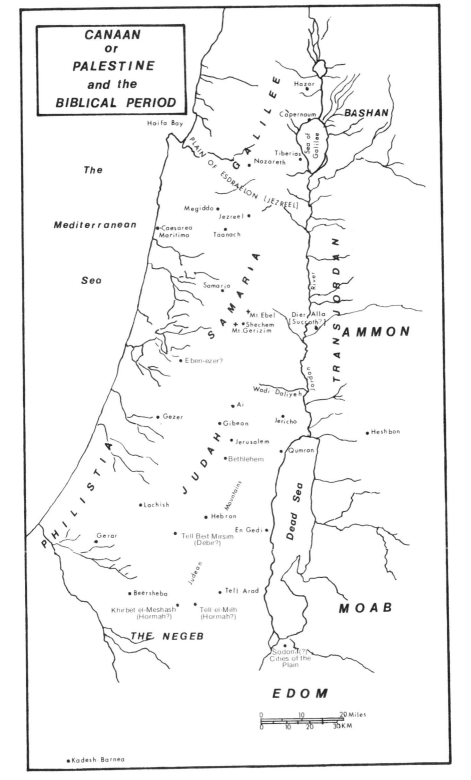

lifetime, although the tradition of worship on Gerizim was evidently still alive. The Samaritan woman reminded Jesus, "Our fathers worshiped on this mountain, while you people say that in Jerusalem is the place where one ought to worship" (John 4:20). An American expedition (R. J. Bull) began excavations at Tell er-Râs in 1964; it has discovered a magnificent temple enclave dedicated to Zeus, constructed by the Emperor Hadrian and approached by a monumental stairway of 1500 steps. Hellenistic buildings from the third century B.C. have been discovered beneath the Roman temple; almost certainly they represent the remnants of the Samaritan temple.[38]

ARAD

All the excavated Palestinian sites considered above after the discussion of Jericho have been to the north of that city. Yet even before the Israelites crossed the Jordan from the east to attack Jericho, they attempted to invade Canaan from the south through the Negeb. A figure who blocked their path was "the Canaanite King of Arad" (Num 21:1; 33:40). Confusingly, a defeat of Israel at nearby Hormah is recorded in Num 14:44-45 and Deut 1:44, while a victory over the King of Arad at Hormah is recorded in Num 21:2-3. The continuing importance of Arad is indicated when, after the conquest of Jericho, Joshua defeated the King of Arad as part of his conquest of the city states of the south (Josh 12:14, a passage which mentions a separate King of Hormah). The settlement of Arad by the Kenite allies of Israel is reported in Judg 1:16.

A valuable contribution of Israeli archaeologists has been the attention they have given to the Negeb or southern

[38]R. J. Bull in BA 31 (1968) 58-72.

desert. In particular, in the 1960s and 1970s Y. Aharoni and Ruth Amiran conducted a major series of excavations at the huge Tell Arad,[39] 18 miles east and slightly north of Beersheba. This Negeb site reflects the difficulty of desert living, for there is no spring; and the cities built there (sometimes as large as 22 acres) have had to depend for water on cisterns or storage basins, facilitated by the presence of waterproof rock. Once again settlement at Arad reaches back to the fourth-millennium Chalcolithic Age and to the first part of the third-millennium Early Bronze Age (with destruction about 2700 B.C.). Even in that early era the influence of the powerful southern neighbor, Egypt, is apparent. What is truly startling is the absence of settlements in the Middle Bronze and Late Bronze Ages, so that the site was unoccupied when, according to the Bible, the Israelites were supposed to be struggling against the King of Arad!

In the Iron Age a twelfth- or eleventh-century settlement, presumably Israelite-dominated from the start, arose at Arad; and 6 strata of occupation, covering as many centuries, have been traced at a citadel-fortress there. Frequent destructions, culminating in a sixth-century catastrophe about the time of the fall of Jerusalem to the Babylonians, bear witness to the strategic importance of Arad for the southern defenses of Judah. A fascinating find in the citadel-fortress is a sanctuary which existed from the 900s to the 600s B.C. On an east-west axis like the Temple of Solomon, this sanctuary had an anteroom with a square altar for burnt offerings. Further west, three steps led up to the Holy of Holies, and on one of the steps stood two pillar-shaped altars with a bowl concavity at the top for holding incense. Within the Holy of Holies there was a vertical stone about a yard in height, rectangular in shape with rounded ends — a massebah. One of the many ostraca

[39]Y. Aharoni in BA 31 (1968) 1-32.

found at Arad (above p. 37) is a letter of about 600 B.C. mentioning the Jerusalem (?) "house of YHWH" — perhaps a challenge to a Yahweh sanctuary that seemingly existed at Arad throughout the reigns of the Davidic monarchs, despite the firm insistence of prophets and preachers in Judah that there should be only one place of worship, the Jerusalem Temple. A multiplicity of sanctuaries was part of the religious policy of the ten-tribe federation that constituted the Kingdom of Israel in the North (I Kings 12:29); but it is shocking to think that a sanctuary could survive in a royal fortress 35 miles south of Jerusalem. And in the Arad house of the aniconic Yahweh there stood one of the stone pillars condemned so vehemently in Deut 16:22; "You shall not set up a *massebah* which the Lord your God hates" (see also I Kings 14:23; II Kings 17:10; 18:4).

In the same vein, at Lachish, some 30 miles southwest of Jerusalem and northwest of Arad, recent excavations have uncovered a series of sanctuaries of Israelite/Jewish provenance, including another Israelite sanctuary of the tenth century B.C.,[40] with altar and lamps; a high place with a massebah stone; and a Jewish temple of *ca.* 200 B.C. When we combine this archaeological information with documentary evidence for the existence of a later Jewish temple at Elephantine (above, p. 38) where seemingly Yahweh was worshiped with a *female consort*, we begin to realize that the standardization of Israelite/Jewish worship was far from complete.

As for the Israelite conquest of Palestine, the formidable problem presented by the absence of second-millennium occupation at Arad before the 1100s has puzzled outstanding Israeli archaeologists. Aharoni, the excavator, argues

---

[40]Lachish had been excavated in the 1930s by J. Starkey, but Israeli archaeologists resumed excavation in the late 1960s (Y. Aharoni) and 1970s (D. Ussishkin).

that in Canaanite times Arad was not at Tell Arad but at Tell el-Milḥ (Malḥata), 7 miles southwest of Tell Arad, while Hormah was at Khirbet el-Meshash (Masos), 3 miles further west. Israeli excavations between 1967 and 1975 have shown that both these sites were occupied in the Middle Bronze Age with a destruction in the 1500s, and that at the second site there was a major Iron Age settlement in the 1200s. Another Israeli scholar, B. Mazar, argues that the Canaanite Arad mentioned in the Bible was an area and that Hormah was a city. He identifies Hormah with Tell el-Milḥ. While either of these solutions is possible, one cannot discuss the Arad issue without reflecting on information from other sites, some of them discussed above.

ARCHAEOLOGY AND OLD TESTAMENT DATING

Perhaps, then, it is time to take stock of difficulties raised by the more accurate archaeological information made available since the Second World War. In particular, let us concentrate on the much debated chronology (and character) of two major biblical eras: the conquest of Canaan, and the time of the Patriarchs.[41]

Israelite Conquest of Canaan. A summary of the pertinent information supplied by the Bible may be useful. Hebrews under Jacob went down from Canaan to Egypt during a famine and were made welcome there because one of their family, Joseph, had become prime minister. Later, there arose a pharaoh who oppressed the people of Israel,

---

[41]See the debate by E. F. Campbell and J. M. Miller in BA 42 (1979) 37-47.

making them do slave labor in building storage cities (Pithom and Raamses). Moses led them out of Egypt after a stay there of 400 or 430 years (Gen 15:13; Exod 12:40). After going to Mount Sinai, they wandered in the desert, with their activity centered at Kadesh-Barnea about 50 miles south of Beersheba. They first tried to enter Canaan from the south through the Negeb but were defeated in whole or in part at Hormah by the Canaanite King of Arad. After 40 years they came up the Transjordan on the eastern side of the Dead Sea, detouring further east around Edom and Moab, but conquering the rulers of Heshbon and Bashan. Joshua led them across the Jordan; he conquered Jericho and pushed into the highlands by conquering Ai. Seemingly without opposition, he went to Shechem to conduct a covenant ceremony at Mounts Ebal and Gerizim. Then Joshua made peace with the Gibeonites; but at Gibeon he defeated a coalition of southern Canaanite kings and conquered their cities, including Lachish, Hebron, and Debir. Next he defeated a coalition of northern kings led by the King of Hazor which he destroyed.

The first reference to Israel in external history is a stele of the Pharaoh Merneptah, *ca.* 1220 B.C., describing victories won in the Canaan area — an indication that by that date Israel was in Canaan. Working back from that reference, many scholars have proposed the following chronology. The Hebrews went to Egypt in the late 1700s at the beginning of the Hyksos era, precisely a time when foreigners descended from Syria into Egypt and ruled the country. Four hundred years later, the Nineteenth Dynasty (Ramses I 1303-1302; Seti I 1302-1290; Ramses II 1290-1224) moved the Egyptian capital to the delta area and began the building projects described in the Bible (city of Raamses) wherein the Hebrews were enslaved labor. The exodus took place in 1300-1280 and by the middle 1200s Israel was in Canaan, as indicated by Merneptah, successor of Ramses II. Albright's dating of the destruction of Jericho to just after 1300 B.C. fitted this theory.

Now, however, we are faced with confusing archaeological evidence, both supportive and contradictory of the biblical evidence. Let me list the archaeological data in the order of names mentioned in the above summary.

— There seems to have been no settlement at Kadesh-Barnea before the tenth century.[42]
— The plausible sites suggested for Hormah were unoccupied from about 1500 to 1200 B.C.
— Tell Arad was unoccupied in the whole period from 2700 to 1100 B.C.[43]
— Heshbon was unoccupied in the second millennium before 1200.
— There was no major city at Jericho after the 1500s.
— Ai was unoccupied from the third millennium to 1200 or later.[44]
— Gibeon was unoccupied from 1500 to 1200 or later.[45]
— There was no major destruction at Hebron (Mamre) in the Late Bronze Age (1550-1200).

On the other hand, two of the Canaanite cities mentioned in the biblical story of the conquest of Canaan were violently destroyed *ca.* 1250-1200, namely Lachish and Hazor

[42]R. Cohen in BA 44 (1981) 93-107.

[43]See the posthumous article on Israel's conquest of the Negeb written by Y. Aharoni in BA 39 (1976) 55-76.

[44]On the 1964-72 excavations see J. Callaway in BA 39 (1976) 18-30. Bethel, near Ai, was destroyed about 1200; but the Bible does not mention a campaign of Joshua against Bethel.

[45]Gibeon was excavated by an American expedition in 1956-1962; see J. B. Pritchard, *Gibeon: Where the Sun Stood Still* (Princeton Univ., 1962). Magnificent water systems were discovered, including an immense pool (see II Sam 2:13).

— also Debir, if it is to be identified with Tell Beit Mirsim. Even then, however, one must be cautious, for a late-thirteenth-century destruction followed by a twelfth-century Israelite occupation does not necessarily mean destruction by Israelites. About this same period the Pharaoh Merneptah was conducting a punitive expedition into Canaan; and there were raids by the Sea Peoples from the Mediterranean, anticipating the Philistine invasion of the next century (*ca.* 1180). One may also note that an important argument for a thirteenth-century date for the exodus has disappeared. Surveys by N. Glueck in the 1930s indicated that Moab was not settled during most of the second millennium before the 1200s; consequently, Israel's avoidance of Moab *en route* to Canaan made no sense before the thirteenth century. Surveys in the 1970s now suggest that the Transjordan was occupied throughout the Late Bronze Age as well (1550-1200).[46]

Such an erosion of evidence for the thirteenth-century Israelite conquest of Palestine has led to much scholarly rethinking. A major figure in this has been G. E. Mendenhall of the University of Michigan.[47] In a radical rewriting of the "conquest" he maintains that there was a massive breakdown of city cultural structure in Palestine at the end of the Late Bronze Age. Israelites did not conquer those cities; indeed, the twelve-tribal federation of Israel took place in Palestine about 1200 only *after* the destruction or collapse of Late Bronze culture. The Israelite "wars" were only guerrilla campaigns by people already on the scene, i.e., of Canaanites influenced by a new religious ideology which led them to attempt a new social organization. Palestinian vil-

---

[46]J. R. Kautz on Moab in BA 44 (1981) 27-35.

[47]G. E. Mendenhall, *The Tenth Generation: The Origins of the Biblical Tradition* (Baltimore: Johns Hopkins, 1973). See also BA 39 (1976) 154-57.

lagers and peasants were led to a struggle to fill in the vacuum created by the Bronze Age collapse; the leaders who purveyed the religious ideology consisted of a small band under the guidance of Moses.

Other forms of rethinking (not necessarily contradictory to Mendenhall's theory) adopt the expedient of interpreting the "conquest" as a composite narrative reflecting a series of events that actually took place over centuries. For instance, if the Hebrews came to Egypt with the Hyksos, many of them may have left with the Hyksos about 1570 B.C. The violent destruction of cities (e.g., Jericho) at the end of the Middle Bronze Age in the mid-1500s, as the shock wave of the Hyksos expulsion rolled back on Palestine, may have reintroduced Hebrews into the land. From the southern desert, tribes akin to the Israelites may have come up through the unoccupied and undefended Negeb in the Late Bronze Age, ultimately giving rise to the House of Judah. The Hapiru raids against the Canaanite city states in the period 1375-1350 mentioned in the Amarna letters (p. 34 above) may have constituted another stratum of what would become Israel. Finally a small band may have come from the Transjordan across the river in the 1200s to serve as a catalytic agent uniting these earlier related groups, somewhat as Mendenhall suggests. In any case, such complicated suggestions show how ambivalent is the claim that archaeology throws light on the Bible.

The Patriarchal Era. In the biblical account a chain of father-son relationships unites Abraham, Isaac, Jacob, and Joseph in four generations. Since Joseph was often seen as figuring in the Hyksos conquest of Egypt in the late 1700s, a date for Abraham in the 1800s was deemed suitable (Middle Bronze IIA). This dating fitted the theory that the patriarchs were part of the Amorite movement. In the east, Amorite waves took over the Sumerian kingdoms of Mesopotamia in the early second millennium, dominating virtually every city state by the eighteenth century. Similarly in the west, Amorites brought to an end the great Early Bronze cities of Palestine and of the Transjordan at the close of the third millennium. The Negeb features prominently in the patriarchal narratives, and Glueck's surveys indicated that the Negeb was occupied between 2000 and 1800, but not much later. Indeed, the picture of Semitic seminomads in an Egyptian tomb-painting at Beni Hasan (1800s) was thought to give an accurate idea of how the patriarchs would have appeared.[48]

Today, the dating of the Patriarchal Era is so disputed that one cannot be sure there is a prevalent opinion any longer.[49] Of course, the intrinsic difficulties in gaining certitude from the biblical information are formidable.[50] In the form known to us, the patriarchal narratives were committed to writing about the tenth century, and we can scarcely expect great historical precision to have been preserved over almost a millennium of popular storytelling. The patriarchs are presented in a family context — scarcely figures likely to leave traces on world history recoverable by archaeology. Virtually all scholars recognize the artificiality of the father-son relationship among the patriarchs. A group for whom Abraham was the revered ancestor may have become allied with a group for whom Isaac was a hero; and the family relationship attributed in the Bible to the patriarchs may thus be an expression of ancient tribal alliances.

If we move on to details, the Beersheba so prominent in the patriarchal narratives (Gen 21:32; 26:23; 28:10) is not

---

[48]W. H. Shea in BA 44 (1981) 219-28.

[49]N. M. Sarna, "Abraham in History," in BARev 3 (#4, 1977) 5-9.

[50]In the Introduction (p. 15) I warned against a fundamentalism which would ignore the conditions that qualify the biblical information and force the interpreter to accept that information literally despite all archaeological evidence to the contrary.

known to have been occupied to any great extent before the Israelite period about 1200. This late dating also affects the well of Beersheba which is essential to the logic of patriarchal occupation. Moreover, the contact between Isaac and a King of the Philistines (Gen 26:1) is anachronistic for a period before 1200. On the other hand, in the first wave of enthusiasm over the Ebla finds, the names associated with Abraham in Genesis 14 were thought to be mentioned in an Early Bronze III context (above, p. 24); and some scholars seem willing to move the patriarchs back 500 years to the 2300s.[51] Others have used the Nuzi parallels to patriarchal practices (above, p. 29) to date the patriarchs to the era when Nuzi flourished, the 1500s,[52] even if that means the truncation of Israel's stay in Egypt. In one form of nineteenth-century scholarship (J. Wellhausen) the patriarchal narratives of Genesis were thought to have minimal or no historical content. They were the compositions of a much later period, and the customs and features of that later period were unconsciously projected back on the distant past. Seemingly one of the contributions of twentieth-century archaeology was to put the stories of Abraham and his descendants on a more solid footing, so that the distinguished archaeologist and biblical scholar, W. F. Albright, could affirm, "There can be little doubt about their substantial historicity."[53] It is ironical that now some scholars, exemplified by T. L. Thompson,[54] would use the problems

[51]Some support this date from excavations in the Gher, south of the Dead Sea, the most plausible site for the "Cities of the Plain" destroyed in the time of Abraham (Gen 19:29); destruction there took place around 2350 and not in the Middle Bronze Age. See W. C. van Hattem in BA 44 (1981) 87-92.

[52]Important is the challenge by J. Van Seters, *Abraham in History and Tradition* (New Haven: Yale, 1975).

[53]BA 36 (1973) 10.

[54]T. L. Thompson, *The Historicity of the Patriarchal Narratives* (New York/Berlin: De Gruyter, 1974).

caused by archaeological discoveries to return to the Well-hausen position. Paradoxically (but with some exaggeration) in this approach much of the Patriarchal Era should be dated to the first millennium when the stories were being "created." However, there are many accuracies in these narratives of the distant past that cannot be so easily explained if the stories are much later creations without an underlying body of reliable tradition. Perhaps "the bottom line" of this discussion is the necessity of greater caution in the use of archaeology both to establish historicity and to dispute it.[55]

If such caution must be exercised in regard to Genesis 12-50, chapters that have a contact with recognizable Middle Eastern and Egyptian history, what is to be said about the prehistory of Genesis 1-11, the stories of the creation and the flood? Some would try to use paleontology to disprove evolution (often on the assumption that the theory of evolution is incompatible with the thesis of a Creator God!). Closer to the theme of this book are the 1955 and 1969 expeditions by Fernand Navarra, a French industrialist, designed to verify the medieval thesis that the resting place of Noah's Ark "upon the mountains of ARRT" (Gen 8:4) refers to Mount Ararat on the Turkish-Russian border,[56] specifically to the extinct volcano called in Turkish Buyuk Aghri Daghi. (There are at least seven other old traditions about the resting place of the Ark, ranging as far as the Arabian peninsula or the mountains of the Tigris region. The Bible probably means the region of Urartu [modern Armenia]; and as the plural "mountains" indicates, it refers to no specific peak.) The search for the Ark presupposes the

---

[55]See the articles on biblical archaeology and history in BA 45 (1982) 201-28.
[56]L. R. Bailey in BA 40 (1977) 137-46; also his *Where is Noah's Ark* (Nashville: Abingdon, 1978).

historicity of the universal flood and the possible survival of a wooden structure from immense antiquity. The fragments of wood brought back from the two expeditions were subjected to radio-carbon dating. The most optimistic dating of the 1955 specimens, reported by Navarra, from Spanish and French laboratories, is in the 4500-5000 year range. That means approximately 3000-2500 B.C. — the Early Bronze Age when *we know* there was no universal flood or even one that covered much of the Middle East! Several English and American laboratories date the specimens from both expeditions much more modestly to A.D. 600-700. No wonder that most biblical scholars refuse to accept the claim that Noah's Ark has been discovered, or to change their view that the Genesis flood story, imaginatively based on local flood stories,[57] is a parabolic vehicle of perceptive theological insight.

DISCOVERIES PERTINENT TO THE NEW TESTAMENT PERIOD

Discussions of archaeological contributions to biblical knowledge devote much more time to the Old Testament than to the New Testament. Israel was a people and a monarchy, leaving indisputable material traces that can be detected by uncovering ancient sites. In the first 100 years of Christian existence (the New Testament Era) the followers of Jesus of Nazareth would have left few remains that can be dug up. Consequently most New Testament archaeology illustrates only the ambiance in which Jesus and his followers would have lived and preached. Already early in the

---

[57]Flood stories are elaborated in various ancient Middle Eastern mythologies; e.g., see T. Frymer-Kensky in BA 40 (1977) 147-55.

twentieth century the travels of Sir William Ramsay[58] showed how the study of the ancient cities that were visited by Paul in his journeys (as described in Acts) and were addressed by letter in the Book of Revelation (the Apocalypse of John) clarified details of the biblical accounts. It should be emphasized, however, that the ambiance information is general in character. It is one thing to see the ruins or excavated remains of a town where Jesus, Peter, or Paul walked; but one must be more skeptical about specific indications related to the lives of these figures, e.g., this is where Jesus multiplied the loaves, or there is a house in which Paul lived. The latter style of identification mostly indicates a place thought worthy by later Christians to recall the memory of such sacred events or persons.

Throughout this century, excavated inscriptions have been published mentioning by title or name some of the officials described in the New Testament. An inscription of special interest was discovered in an Israeli excavation in 1961 at Caesarea on the Mediterranean coast, a Herodian city that became the Roman administrative headquarters. Derived from a building dedicated to the Emperor Tiberius, the inscription has the designation "Pontius Pilate, Prefect of Judea," and thus confirms the suspicion of scholars that Tacitus (*Annals* 15.44) was anachronistic when he called Pilate a procurator, a title not used for the Palestinian governor before the time of Claudius.

Often, too, the discoveries have cast light on customs mentioned in the New Testament. For instance, Mark 7:9-13 reports that Jesus criticized the Pharisees and scribes for freeing someone from an obligation toward a parent if the person said, "Anything of mine that might have been of use

[58]W. W. Gasque, *Sir William M. Ramsay* (Grand Rapids: Eerdmans, 1966). BAR 2. 313-420 gathers various BA articles on New Testament cities.

to you is *Qorban*." From later rabbinic usage, most scholars understood the statement to refer to dedicating gifts to God. Now the inscribed lid of a Jewish ossuary (bone box) discovered in the 1950s in a Kidron Valley tomb from the beginning of the Christian Era[59] has these words, "All that a person may find of profit in this ossuary is *Qorban* to God from the one who lies within it." The New Testament (Matt 16:18; Mark 3:16; John 1:42) agrees that Jesus changed the designation of one of his followers, Simon bar-Jona, to Kepha (Aramaic) or Petros (Greek), meaning "rock"; but we have never been certain whether this was a nickname or whether Simon was the first person to bear it. Now, J. A. Fitzmyer[60] has pointed to a pre-Christian reference to a Semite (probably a Jew) named "Aqab, son of Kepha" in the Elephantine documents (above, pp.37-38).

On a more somber note, despite Jewish and Christian references to crucifixion, we have never had firsthand evidence of that gruesome punishment. Recently, there have been published two Dead Sea texts mentioning the hanging of men to die on a tree, the same expression used of Jesus in Acts 5:30, "whom you killed by hanging on a tree" (see also 10:39). More important is the discovery in 1968 of the bones of a crucified man[61] in a first-century A.D. tomb near Mount Scopus (Jerusalem). Although there is some debate about the exact position of the man during crucifixion as implied by the bones, it is clear that the two nails used for the hands were actually driven through the wrists. One nail seems to have been used to attach the two legs to the cross

---

[59] J. A. Fitzmyer, *Essays on the Semitic Background of the New Testament* (London: Chapman, 1971; Missoula, Montana: Scholars Press, 1974) 93-100.

[60] J. A. Fitzmyer, *To Advance the Gospel* (New York: Crossroad, 1981) 115-18.

[61] *Ibid.* 125-46.

Possible Position of a Man during Crucifixion

"Although there is some debate about the exact position of the man during crucifixion as implied by the bones, it is clear that the two nails used for the hands were actually driven through the wrists".

"One nail seems to have been used to attach the two legs to the cross together through the heel bone, and the legs of the crucified were broken (John 19:32)."

Spike-Pierced Heel Bones

together through the heel bone, and the legs of the crucified were broken (John 19:32). In this century there was published an inscription discovered at Nazareth containing an ordinance of the Emperor (probably Claudius, A.D. 41-54), insisting that graves must remain intact and instituting the death penalty for anyone who would violate a burial place. The time of the inscription and locale where it was found raised in the minds of some scholars the suspicion that the charges and countercharges about stealing the body of Jesus of Nazareth (Matt 28:11-15) may have contributed to such governmental concern for tombs.

Such finds cast general light on the death and burial of Jesus. Much more problematic is the claim that the Shroud of Turin is the actual burial cloth of Jesus.[62] This curious image (almost the equivalent of a photographic negative) of a deceased man corresponds to the accounts of the wounds of Jesus preserved in *different* gospels. Careful modern tests show that it was not painted, and no one has been able to prove exactly how the image was produced. The Shroud can be traced with surety back to the Middle Ages (precisely a time when returning Crusaders created a passion for relics from the Holy Land) but is said to betray a knowledge of anatomy not available at that time. There are botanical signs that once the cloth had been in Palestine. Uncertain is the claim that the Shroud of Turin is identical with a much earlier cloth (seemingly lost by A.D. 1000) called the Mandylion of Edessa which bore a facial image of the crucified Christ. There was first-century contact between Jerusalem and Edessa, so that a Jerusalem-Edessa-Crusader-France itinerary is possible. The Shroud has never been subjected to radio-carbon dating. The claim that a coin of Pontius Pilate covers one of the eyes of the figure on the Shroud of Turin is difficult to verify even when the photo is greatly magnified.[63] In the 1350s when the shroud appeared in France in the possession of Geoffrey de Charny, it was clearly thought by the local bishops of the area to be a reproduction rather than the actual shroud of Christ; and someone is said to have admitted making it. Overall, two observations must be made. If it is a forgery, it is one of the cleverest of all times, baffling even the best tests of modern science. If it is genuine, it tells us virtually nothing about Christ's death that is not already known from the Scriptures. As for Christian faith, those who receive the blessing of John 20:29 for

[62]I. Wilson, *The Shroud of Turin: the Burial Cloth of Jesus Christ?* (Garden City, NY: Doubleday, 1978); Virginia Borten in BA 43 (1980) 109-17; K. F. Weaver supplies excellent photographs in *National Geographic* 157 (June 1980) 730-52. For the science, see J. H. Heller, *Report on the Shroud of Turin* (Boston: Houghton Mifflin, 1983).

[63]See the debate in BA 43 (1980) 112, 197; 44 (1981) 135-37.

believing in Jesus without seeing his risen body will scarcely
need the support of having seen an image of his dead body,
however that image was produced.

Having surveyed some general contributions of archaeology to New Testament background, let us turn now briefly
to some specific sites.

JERUSALEM

Naturally, the most famous city in the Bible has attracted
many excavators, beginning already in the 1860s with C.
Warren. There is the usual problem that the half-dozen digs
done before 1925 did not have the technological skills to
interpret correctly their finds. Another difficulty is that
Jerusalem has been continually occupied since its seizure by
David *ca.* 1000; and constant rebuildings have made interpretation fiendishly difficult even for the most modern technology. Moreover, much of Jerusalem is sacred ground to
three religions, Jewish, Christian, Moslem, either because
of holy places or of burials; and often the very area that
would be the most interesting or the most necessary for
clarifying stratigraphy cannot be excavated. Kathleen
Kenyon[64] turned to Jerusalem (1961-1967) after her
extraordinary success at Jericho, only to be plagued by a
final problem, i.e., war. The 1967 campaign by Israel took
Old Jerusalem from the Jordanians; this change caused
Kenyon to interrupt her dig, never to resume it. Since 1967
Israeli archaeologists have been very active in different
sections of the city.[65]

The most eye-catching feature of Old Jerusalem even
today is the enclosure that once surrounded the Temple and

[64]K. M. Kenyon, *Digging up Jerusalem* (London: Praeger, 1979).
[65]*Jerusalem Revealed*, ed. Y. Yadin (New Haven: Yale, 1976).

now surrounds the beautiful Moslem sanctuary of the
Dome of the Rock. The oldest section of the city (the
Jebusite or Canaanite citadel conquered by David) lay
south of this enclosure; and there has been a major archaeological effort[66] to unravel the complexities of that area
including the city defensive walls, the tombs of the kings of
Judah, and the water supply channels. Excavation has
brought some clarity and inevitably some disappointments.
The theory that the shaft discovered by Warren in the last
century was the *ṣinnor* (tunnel?) by which David entered the
Canaanite city has now been disproved. Many more campaigns may be necessary before scholars agree on the history
of this portion of Jerusalem, and for the non-specialist its
jumble of walls will probably always remain an unattractive
mystery.

When Solomon built the Temple, the city spread north on
the east side flanking the Kidron valley. The *exact* location
of the Temple of Solomon (First Temple, *ca.* 960-587 B.C.),
which has not left any physical remains, has been the subject
of much discussion; but some light was cast by recent excavations on the location of the walls of the Second Temple
(515-A.D. 70).[67] Seemingly and surprisingly this Temple
was not under the present Dome of the Rock but to the
north of it. A major historical question involves the date
when the city spread from the eastern side to the western
hill, which is actually the highest spot in Old Jerusalem and
to which the name Mount Zion was eventually given.
Apparently this major expansion which made Jerusalem
truly a city happened in the eighth century, partly in connec-
tion with the fall of Samaria and the Northern Kingdom of
Israel in 721 B.C.[68] Refugees streamed to the south and
Jerusalem became their haven.

[66]Articles by Y. Shiloh in BA 42 (1979) 165-71; 44 (1981) 161-70.
[67]A. S. Kaufman in BA 44 (1981) 108-15.
[68]M. M. Eisman in BA 41 (1978) 49-53.

Without neglecting such finds from the older period of Jerusalem's history, one must admit that the most interesting recent discoveries have cast light on the last century B.C. and the first century A.D.[69] In particular, the buildings of the Hasmonean priests and of the Herodian kings have become more visible and are truly impressive. It was known that *ca.* 20 B.C. Herod the Great began reconstruction projects on the Second Temple; by the time of Jesus' ministry (John 2:20) the project had already been in progress for 46 years! Israeli excavations have uncovered the southern and western walls and the entrances of the Herodian Temple enclosure,[70] making it clear that Jesus' disciples were not exaggerating when they exclaimed, "Look, Teacher, what wonderful stones and what wonderful buildings" (Mark 13:1). Walls made of precisely fitted stones of immense size, colonnaded porticoes (stoa), double and triple gateways approached by monumental steps, a bridge over the valley dividing the eastern and western hills, and paved streets underneath — these have all been uncovered in whole or in part. It becomes apparent that Herod rivaled Solomon himself in the expenditure of wealth and the grandeur of design. The warnings of Jesus and of other first-century Jewish voices that all this could be destroyed seem more audaciously prophetic, now that we see the imposing solidity of what stood before their eyes.

Major remnants of a Hasmonean/Herodian fortress-palace (named the Antonia after Mark Anthony) that was situated just north of the Temple area were identified (a bit too enthusiastically) in the last century. A pavement of massive stone slabs recalled the *lithostrotos* or "Stone Pavement" in John 19:13, and led some scholars to argue that the

---

[69]Very careful in evaluating evidence is J. Wilkinson, *Jerusalem as Jesus Knew It* (London: Thames and Hudson, 1978).

[70]B. Mazar in BARev 6 (#4, 1980), 44-59.

Artist's Reconstruction of the Temple Area
in Herod's Jerusalem

It was known that *ca.* 20 B.C. Herod the Great began reconstruction projects on the Second Temple; by the time of Jesus' ministry (John 2:20) the project had already been in progress for 46 years! Israeli excavations have uncovered the southern and western walls and the entrances of the Herodian Temple enclosure, making it clear that Jesus' disciples were not exaggerating when they exclaimed, "Look, Teacher, what wonderful stones and what wonderful buildings" (Mark 13:1).

The Temple Mount in Jerusalem

Herodian pavement and steps at the foot of the south wall, showing the depth below present ground level.

Antonia served as the praetorium (18:28) or Roman guber-
natorial headquarters where Pilate tried Jesus. It now seems
more likely that the stone slabs are from the Roman city of
Aelia Capitolina constructed on the site of Jerusalem a
century later, in Hadrian's time. An arch, dubbed "Ecce
Homo" because it was thought to be the site from which
Pilate showed Jesus to the crowd (19:5), is now judged to be
part of the eastern city gate built by Herod Agrippa I, a
decade after Jesus' time. Another candidate for the praetorium is a palace-fortress on the west hill (Mount Zion), the
Citadel near the Jaffa Gate.[71] Recent excavations have
helped to clarify the extent of the palace and its impressive
towers.

Connected to the identification of the Citadel towers is
the issue of the northern wall of Jerusalem during Jesus'
time. Josephus describes a history of three defensive walls
(perhaps too modest a numbering!), the first of which was
built long before by David and Solomon, and the third of
which was begun by Herod Agrippa I in the 40s after Jesus'
lifetime.[72] The Second Wall would have been standing during Jesus' ministry; it included more of the city than did the
first but much less than did the third. Golgotha or Calvary,
"the Place of the Skull" where Jesus died, stood outside that
Second Wall, as did his nearby tomb (John 19:20, 41-42). In
the early fourth century Constantine built the Church of the
Resurrection or Holy Sepulchre on the site then venerated
by Christians as the place of death and of burial; it stands
well within the modern (Turkish) city walls. Some scholars
who have identified those walls with the approximate line of
the Second Wall reject the authenticity of the Holy
Sepulchre. (From Edward Robinson on, discussions of the
burial place of Jesus have not been uninfluenced by the

[71]M. Broshi in BA 40 (1977) 11-17.
[72]E. W. Hamrick in BA 40 (1977) 18-23.

dislike of many Westerners for the appearance of the Church of the Holy Sepulchre and for the religious rivalries that mar it.) Recent discoveries make it likely that the Second Wall (built by the Hasmonean priests *ca.* 100 B.C. or later by Herod?) came east from one of the towers of the Herodian Citadel and ran south of what now is the site of the Sepulchre which, consequently, was well outside the wall.[73] Indeed, it seems as if much of the area around the Sepulchre was a quarry from which stones for the wall were hewed. The knoll called Golgotha may have been left unquarried because of the poor quality of the stone and/or because it was split by an earthquake. Tombs were frequently cut into areas left standing in a quarry, and one of the tombs thus cut could have belonged to Joseph of Arimathea, as the Scriptures report. Archaeology cannot verify the place of Jesus' death and burial, but the claim that archaeology has disproved the authenticity of the Holy Sepulchre may now be dropped.

NAZARETH AND CAPERNAUM

Evidence about other sites of Jesus' life is hard to interpret. There has been considerable modern debate about the historicity of the infancy narratives in Matthew and in Luke, in particular about the likelihood of his birth at Bethlehem. In antiquity, however, those infancy stories would have been accepted and embellished. The Church of the Nativity was built by Constantine (A.D. 326) over a cave already venerated as the site of the birth events. Jerome (*Epistle 58, to Paulinus*) reports that in Hadrian's time

---

[73]R. H. Smith in BA 30 (1967) 74-90; reprinted in BAR 3. 390-404; B. F. Schein in BA 44 (1981) 21-26.

(A.D. 135) the Romans had here a grove in honor of Tammuz (Adonis): "In the grove where the Christ-Child once cried they wept for Venus' lover." But even if the rival Roman cult shows that there was a Christian sacred site here some 140 years after Christ's birth, one must still decide whether the site represented historical memory or was simply the localization of a pious belief.

At Nazareth important excavations have been conducted by B. Bagatti since 1955 in relation to the rebuilding of the Church of the Annunciation. Under a fifth-century Byzantine church there was an earlier church with the measurements attested elsewhere for Jewish synagogues. This similarity causes the excavators to speak of a church-synagogue frequented by Jewish Christians. At the same site several caves served as places of Christian devotion. The oldest known inscription with the Greek words for "Hail Mary" was found, as well as an inscription to "Christ, Son of God." It has been urged that such devotion probably reflects a memory of the house of Mary and of a cave which was the site of the angelic annunciation (Luke 1:26-27). What is certain from the excavations, however, is that this is a site in Mary's hometown where her memory was venerated by Christians from an early period.

The impressive synagogue ruins standing at Capernaum on the northern shore of the Lake of Galilee have been the object of debate. Is this the synagogue in which Jesus healed and preached (Mark 1:21; John 6:59) or is it a later synagogue perhaps built over the first-century synagogue? Many scholars think that the existing synagogue is of the third century A.D., but excavations since 1968 (V. Corbo) indicate an even later date (fourth century). Just south of the synagogue, closer to the lake, is an octagonal fifth-century church; but under it the excavators found signs of several centuries of buildings honoring Peter, going back to what they claim was a first-century house that was turned into a Jewish-Christian place of cult. In their judgment they have found the house of Peter mentioned in Mark 1:29 which Jesus entered when he left the synagogue. At least, one may judge that the excavations at Nazareth and Capernaum conducted by the Franciscan Fathers are revealing that a form of Jewish Christianity lasted in Galilee for several centuries with remarkable continuity.[74]

ROME

The Peter whose home was at Capernaum died in|Rome in the 60s — almost all scholars would agree on that today. Under the site of the present St. Peter's Church, Constantine had a basilica built in A.D. 333. Excavations begun in the 1940s under the Constantinian level of the church have yielded fascinating discoveries.[75] This Vatican hill outside the ancient city was the site of the Circus of Nero; it was also a burial ground for rich and poor. The wealthy had mausoleums, but adjacent to the mausoleums was a place where burial was by simply inhumation. The Constantinian architects leveled part of the hill, and their buildings cut into the mausoleums. The modern excavations have uncovered streets of a pagan necropolis going back as far as A.D. 70-100. The high altar of St. Peter's Church was over a spot where there were no mausoleums. About A.D. 160, a retaining wall, dubbed the red wall, was built in order to terrace the area. Near the center of that wall and directly under the subsequent high altar, there was a series of 3 superimposed niches, the upper two of which were part of the wall, the lowest of which was underground — a trench-like cavity cut

[74]Both the archaeological evidence and its evaluation may be found in B. Bagatti, *The Church from the Circumcision* (Jerusalem: Franciscan Press, 1971).

[75]R. T. O'Callaghan in BA 12 (1949) 1-23; 16 (1953) 70-87.

across at an angle by the wall. The upper two were the focus of a shrine or memorial consisting of a travertine stone slab resting on two marble columns and built against the wall. There is little doubt that this was the *tropaion* (trophy, memorial, perhaps tomb) referred to by the Roman presbyter Gaius, when *ca.* A.D. 200 he bragged about Rome's heritage from Peter and Paul: "I can show you the 'trophies' of the apostles. For whether you go to the Vatican, or along the Ostian Way, you will find the 'trophies' of those who founded the Church of Rome" (Eusebius, *History* 2.25.7).

Was the lowest niche a grave that once contained the bones of Peter?[76] One might guess that Peter was martyred in the Circus of Nero, that his friends exercised their legal right to ask for his body, and that they buried it nearby in an area where the poor were inhumed. They would have had to remember and even to mark the site of the burial and then 100 years later, when it was possible, to build a monument. Although bones (seemingly those of two men and a woman) were found in an indentation under the red wall, no bones were found in the lowest niche. Accordingly, Pope Pius XII stated on December 23, 1950 that it was impossible to identify the remains of Peter in these excavations. However, about A.D. 250 another wall was built at a right angle to the end of the red wall and in that supporting wall was inserted a marble box, near which a graffito or inscription mentioned Peter. When this marble box was opened publicly, it contained only debris with minuscule bone fragments. Years later Professor Margherita Guarducci claimed that it had previously been opened privately during the Second World War and that the bones of an elderly man which it contained had been deposited in another place in the Vatican. It was argued that these bones were originally in the lowest niche in

[76]G. F. Snyder in BA 32 (1969) 1-24. J. E. Walsh, *The Bones of St. Peter* (Garden City, NY: Doubleday, 1982).

the red wall and that they had been put in the marble box when they were moved to be inserted in the later supporting wall. We would then both have the bones of Peter and know his original burial place which was already venerated in A.D. 160. Pope Paul VI accepted this thesis on June 26, 1968.

Nevertheless there are major difficulties facing it. (1) There is no way to verify the story that the marble box once contained bones. (2) It is not clear whether the *tropaion* of the second century marked the burial place, or the place of martyrdom, or was simply a memorial to Peter near where he died — the site of the monument being determined by availability instead of by historical memory. (3) There is a rival tradition at another place in Rome; for on the Appian Way in antiquity there stood a "Basilica of the Apostles" at a site associated with St. Sebastian. Several inscriptions there mention Peter and Paul; but especially important is an inscription by Pope Damasus (*ca.* 375): "Whoever you are who seek the names of Peter and Paul, you must know that here the saints once dwelled." Since this site does not seem to have been a place for private dwelling, does the inscription refer to the resting place of the bodies of the Apostles? One might argue that the bones of Peter were taken from the niche in the Vatican wall in the mid-third century because of persecutions and were later returned to the Vatican, being placed in the marble box. But this theory raises as many problems as it solves in terms of motive and procedure.

Perhaps all that one can conclude is that Gentile Christians in Rome, even as Jewish Christians in Galilee, began very quickly to select memorial places where they could do honor to figures who surrounded Jesus in the Gospel narrative, such as Mary and Peter. The lives and sometimes the deaths of such figures had now become part of the Christian story and were to be commemorated by holy places.

* * *

This *selection* of documentary and archaeological discoveries illustrates recent gains in knowledge pertinent to the Bible. A review of the biblical applications suggested above shows how scholars, working inductively from such discoveries, have been able to cast light on almost every aspect of both Testaments: canonical collection, scribal transmission, languages, writing style, history, life-patterns, theology, worship, etc. To "cast light" on anything clarifies some features but brings out rough spots and awkwardness that otherwise would not have been visible. To some, the difficulties or problems uncovered by modern scholarship detract from the beauty of the sacred page which, in their view, should not be marred by human imperfections. To others, what has been uncovered by scholarship, including the problems, confirms the appropriateness of the Bible as the basic text of two religions, Judaism and Christianity, which in different ways have insisted that the truly human is a proper sphere or vehicle for the revelation of the truly divine.

SUGGESTIONS FOR FURTHER READING

The footnotes are meant to offer more reading, usually of a less-technical nature. Among works of a readable but more technical nature are the following:

The Jerome Biblical Commentary, ed. R. E. Brown *et al.* (Englewood Cliffs, NJ: Prentice-Hall, 1968), general articles on history, archaeology, canonicity, texts and versions.

Encyclopaedia of Archaeological Excavations in the Holy Land, ed. M. Avi-Yonah (London: Oxford, 1975-1978). Excellent on individual sites.

Interpreter's Dictionary of the Bible, Supplementary Volume (Nashville: Abingdon, 1976). This 5th volume updates sites discussed in the first four.

Archaeology (Israel Pocket Library; Jerusalem: Keter, 1971). Articles from the *Encyclopaedia Judaica* on the most important sites.

Pritchard, J. B., *Ancient Near East Texts* (rev. ed.; Princeton Univ., 1955). Offers translations of most of the tablets and texts I discussed, relative to the Old Testament.

Murphy-O'Connor, J., *The Holy Land: An Archaeological Guide from Earliest Times to 1700* (Oxford Univ., 1980). Concise and up-to-date.

Hayes, J. H. and J. M. Miller, eds., *Israelite and Judaean History* (Old Testament Library; Philadelphia: Westminster, 1977).

Aharoni, Y., *The Land of the Bible: A Historical Geography* (Philadelphia: Westminster, 1967).

Albright, W. F., *The Archaeology of Palestine* (rev. ed.; Baltimore: Penguin, 1960).

Albright, W. F., *From the Stone Age to Christianity* (2nd ed.; Garden City, NY: Doubleday Anchor, 1957).

INDEX